Modern Collector's Dolls

Eighth Series

Patricia R. Smith

COLLECTOR BOOKS
A Division of Schroeder Publishing Co., Inc.

The current values in this book should be used only as a guide. They are not intended to set prices, which vary from one section of the country to another. Auction prices as well as dealer prices vary greatly and are affected by condition as well as demand. Neither the Author nor the Publisher assumes responsibility for any losses that might be incurred as a result of consulting this guide.

Searching For A Publisher?

We are always looking for knowledgeable people considered to be experts within their fields. If you feel that there is a real need for a book on your collectible subject and have a large comprehensive collection, contact Collector Books.

Cover design by Beth Summers
Book layout by Karen Geary

⮑ Dedication ⮐

I deeply and sincerely dedicate this volume to two people without whom I could not work – Mr. Bill Schroeder, publisher and friend, who has helped me, always; and Karen Geary, the editor who has worked with me for a number of years. We both put in just about as many hours, have just about the same plateau of aggravation and tension, and sigh just about the same depth of relief when our work is done.
To both my love and respect.

Credits

Gloria Anderson, Chaye Arotsky, Betty Barclift, Sandy Johnson Barts, Sally Bethschieder, Ken Bowers, Kay Bransky, Geri Cotes, Connie Diehl, Ellen Dodge, Doll Cradle, Marie Ernst, Diane French (Grand Lady Museum, Chance Pond, West Franklin, NH 03235), Maureen Fukishima, LeeAnn Geary, Susan Girardot (05431 State Route 119, Minster, OH 45865), Pat Graff, Joan Guelzov, Amanda Hash, Lee Nell Hayes, Carmen Holshoe, Steve Humphries, Floyd & Gracie James, Carl Jankech, Joan's Treasured Dolls (337 Central St., Franklin, NH 03243), Cris Johnson, Roger Jones, Phyllis & Cecil Kates, Jo Keelan, Diane Kornhauser, Joane Knoedler, Theo Lindley, Kris Lundquist, Barbara Male, Margaret Mandel, Cyndie Matus, Jeannie Mauldin, Ellyn McCorkell, Sharon McDowell, Chris McWilliams, Claudia Meeker, Elizabeth Montesano, Harold Naber (Naber Gestalt Corp., 8915 S. Suncoast Blvd., Homosassa, FL 34446), Jeannie Nespoli, Randy Numley, Mel Odom, Anita Pacey, Peggy Pergande, Pat Pratt, Doris Rickert, Evelyn Samec, Dale R. Schell, Marion Schmuhl, June Schultz, Cindy Shaffer, Linda Shelton, Betty Shriver, Charmaine Shields, Shirley's Doll House (P.O. Box 99, Wheeling, IL 60090) Jessie Smith, Judith Smith, Virginia Sofie, Pat Sparks, Paul Spencer (1414 Clover Leaf, Waco, TX 76705), David Spurgeon, Helena Street, Karen Stevenson, Bonnie Stewart, Beth Summers, Martha Sweeney, Andrew Tabbat, Charleen Thanos, Kathy Tvrdik, Turn Of Century Antiques (1475 Broadway, Denver, CO 80210), Marjorie Uhl, Jeanne Venner, Ann Wilhite, Mary Williams, Edith Wise, Cecilia White, Carol J. Wetheria, Patricia Wood, Glorya Woods.

Cover Photo Credit

TONI, marked P-93, with very hard-to-find black nylon wig. Made by Ideal Toy Corporation. $500.00 up. ELISE Balleria made in 1958 by Madame Alexander. $450.00. 14" TONI BALLERINA and 8" BETSY MCCALL dolls made by American Character Company. $285.00 and $200.00. In riding habit - $450.00. *Courtesy Pat Smith. Photo by Dwight Smith.*

Note

In this book, there may be dolls that have been previously shown in the *Doll Values* series. There could be dolls that have appeared in the *Modern Collector's Dolls* series, but they will be pictured in different outfits or in costumes that need to be seen in color to be appreciated. Prices are based on near mint, clean, original dolls with the exception of Madame Alexander dolls whose prices reflect perfect, mint dolls.

⌒ Contents ⌒

Preface

1995 has been a "ho-hum" year. A vast number of collectors/dealers remember back to the time they were "closet collectors" of modern dolls. It does not seem that long ago, but it was a quarter of a century or more. Those were the the "ho" years when your friends and relatives thought that you had become senile.

The "hum" years began in 1974 when there was a doll "boom," and hobbists were finding just about anything they wanted. During this same time, the inception of doll shows occured. Prior to that, there was only one doll business, Kimport Dolls, that traveled with their wares. Their main concern was antique dolls, but they also carried modern dolls made in foreign countries. Also during this time, publications featuring antiques and collectibles ran more and more doll advertisements. Before long, an all doll publication was born, then another, and yet another.

The 1970s went "humming" along with thousands of collectors being born. Soon the thrift shops' supplies dried up and more and more attics were cleaned out of childhood dolls. It is no wonder that the prices rose during this period. As prices climbed and collections grew, collectors themselves became dealers, selling lesser dolls to be able to upgrade their collection. Collectors also realized they would have to be a dealer to get into doll shows early as the other dealers were able to get all the bargains before the doors opened to the public. Hence, more doll shows.

During the 1970s, Madame Alexander dolls became an insatiable desire for more and more collectors, and the company was not geared to handle the demand. As collectors placed their names on waiting lists for that year's dolls, many friendships went by the wayside and downright battles carried over to the 1980s and 1990s. Prices of Madame Alexander dolls doubled on the secondary market, then rose even higher. Yes, the antique market was doing the same thing. Here are two examples: An Alexander 21" "Coco" Portrait rose from $100.00 to $1,000.00. At the same time, a 17" closed mouth French Jumeau climbed from $700.00 to $2,200.00.

What about Barbie? During the "hum" years, it was "ho" for Barbie. Collectors pushed her aside in thrift shops to search for other dolls. Barbie appeared in these shops as children finished playing with her. Thrift shops had so many of these dolls in 1978 that they lumped them into sacks with handfuls of clothes and sold them for $2.00. This brings up a point of interest. Dolls that have been *played with* and/or made for the *child's* market will be the *only* Barbies being searched for in years to come. "Those cheap things?" you ask. "No, those non-available things!" you will be answered. All the other Barbie dolls are being kept *mint in the box,* and because one dealer wanted to make more money, he invented the NRFB – *Never Removed From Box*. This dealer has published that whenever Barbie is removed from her box, her value is decreased by 50%! These dolls will be around and available to anyone for hundreds of years, or for as long they survive. By keeping dolls sealed in their boxes, no one knows what will happen to the vinyl, clothes, or hair.

Barbie dolls that have been played with and are considered thrift shop quality will be the collectible dolls in the future. Mattel has left the children's market alone and has concentrated on the collectible market by making "series dolls." If you have one doll in the series, it is natural for you to want all of the dolls in that set. Other companies have used this same merchandising tactic, and it continues to be a popular marketing strategy.

By end of the 1970s, avid collectors were shaking their heads, wondering what had happened in the doll world. The days of fun and games were over. Dolls were a very serious business now. A new element was added to the collecting field – *investment*. Suddenly, the enjoyment of collecting diminished, and only a few individuals purchased dolls just because they liked a particular doll. More than 15 years have passed since investment dolls made by various companies were purchased, and now collectors of those dolls are receiving a rude awakening when they try to "cash in." They are shocked to learn that the investments are worth approximately what they paid for the dolls years ago – or less.

By the early 1980s, a deep, saddening recession attacked the doll collecting field. Cabbage Patch had begun another frenzy of fad spending. That company fell into the trap of over-producing and then letting the supply meet the demand – thereby causing financial disaster. This method of corporate suicide has been used by many companies, and sadly, it will continue to occur for years to come.

Times change, many collections have new ownership, or individual dolls have been sold. Collectors who entered the doll field since 1982 have encountered the high-priced market, and they continue to see doll prices escalate. Those collectors have adjusted to the market and continue to spend what they can on their dolls. Collecting will continue and survive, but it is hoped that one day the hobby will return to just that – a hobby – not a business and emotional hard work. There is enough tension in our world without our hobby being stressful.

This interesting note may answer many questions about some dolls. From the late 1940s to the mid-1950s, merchandise from companies was on a franchise basis. This meant no one put items on sale unless all did at the same time or the store would lose its franchise. The only thing that came close to a discount store was Sears and Montgomery Wards. It was not until the late 1950s and early 1960s that self-service and discount stores came into being on a nationwide scale.

During those franchise years, a few doll companies made "secret" dolls which were to be discounted for catalog firms. The dolls were nearly the same, but the clothes were of lesser quality, yet with the same styling. Among these were the Ⓧ marked composition dolls and the marked "backward 21" dolls.

These dolls came from two of the best known makers of the time – Madame Alexander and Ideal Toys.

Also in the 1950s, there was a serious need to compete with new products – many of which were by-products of the World War II era. Three major doll companies who could not afford to manufacture their own dolls contracted with Kodac Injection Moulding to produce all of their undressed dolls. Designer Bernard Lipfert was hired to develop the doll heads. The heads varied slightly, but the bodies were identical. Reduced versions of these same molds are marked "Made in USA/14" and were sold to anyone wanting to buy doll "blanks" to dress and market.

As vinyl became more usable and cost effective, and plastic became readily available, many of the same mould companies continued to make blanks for anyone who wanted to pro-

13" all composition "McGuffey Ana" style doll marked with "Ⓧ" mark. *Courtesy June Schultz.*

duce dolls under their own name. The most common of these dolls, and the most obtainable for collectors, is the "14R" marked doll with an adult body and high-heeled feet. Another style of blank has the "AE" mark plus a number. This represents the "jobber-customer" number. When the company order number is known, the collector can tell which company dressed and marketed the doll. Among the "AE" marked dolls are adults, children of all descriptions, and babies. Some of the doll making companies were Frisch Doll Co., Plastic Moulded Arts, Commonwealth, Doll Bodies, Natural Doll Co., M.C. Doll Co., Ontario Plastics, Paris Dolls, and even Horsman Dolls and Ideal Dolls.

Left: This is a typical example of the vinyl "14R" doll that was sold to companies that dressed and marketed their own doll products. *Courtesy Kathy Tvrdik.*

Below: The 14" hard plastic doll on the left was made by Frisch Doll Co. and marked "Made in USA." The doll on the right is a 14" hard plastic "Mary Hoyer" doll. As you can see, they are identical. *Courtesy Kris Lundquist.*

Madame Alexander

Modern collectors tend to forget that Madame Alexander dolls were developed and marketed mainly for the more affluent families and friends to give to their favorite child. The dolls were sold through exclusive children's clothing stores and large expensive department stores such as Wanamaker's, FAO Schwarz, Saks Fifth Avenue, and May Company.

It's true that Madame Alexander dolls appeared in major catalog stores like Sears & Roebucks and Montgomery Wards, but the dolls were still expensive. Nevertheless, these mail-order companies were reaching clientele they had always tried to obtain – consumers who could afford to spend extra. Soon, Sears and Wards began using name brand products in all aspects of their catalog to attract this same customer population.

The general public is very realistic and bypass the current high-priced Madame Alexander dolls. Instead, they head for the discount children's stores and select the lower, but still inflated, priced dolls available. In other words, to the noncollector, Madame Alexander dolls remain where they have always been – in the "for the rich" price bracket.

Collectors are accustomed to high prices. In fact, $56.00 plus tax is acceptable for an 8" doll *not to be played with*. By contrast, the general public will pay $9.95 to $36.95 for dolls *to be played with*. If proof is needed, look at the baby dolls in toy stores or discount stores such as K-Mart, Wal-Mart, Venture, and others. Then take a look at any Madame Alexander baby priced $94.95 to $124.95. There is no comparison! (There are a few Alexander babies priced $39.95, but they are meant for play.)

Whenever I conducted appraisal clinics throughout the United States and someone brought in a Madame Alexander doll from their childhood, I would let them know how fortunate they were to have a parent or relative who was able to purchase their doll. Prices for such dolls were far greater than the majority of dolls from other makers.

Let us take a look at the "Madeline" doll of 1952. She was 18" tall, made of hard plastic, and had extra joints at the knees and elbows. All of this was a costly way to make a doll. The quality of the clothes matched the finest adult clothes designed.

Now let us look at Madeline's lavish lifestyle. The following descriptions can be found in the brochure showing the extra clothing that could be purchased. (It must be remembered that the little girl that owned her is named Lucy.)

LAST DAY OF SCHOOL: Each child is to bring their favorite best dressed doll to school. Lucy takes Madeline dressed in white dress and bright red pinafore. She won the prize! A picture of two dresses are shown on this page (and it is pointed out that Madeline would have won in either outfit.)

A BEAUTIFUL AFTERNOON: Lucy's mother has baked a cake for Grandmother's birthday and she always visited for early tea on this day. For this special occasion, Lucy dressed up, and she also clothed Madeline in one of her finest dresses – a lavender one. Madeline hopes she can go to another birthday soon so she can wear the other dress that came in white, pink, or blue shown on that page.

MADELINE GOES TO A PICNIC: Lucy has a visiting friend, and both girls watch as Cook packs a wonderful basket for the picnic. Madeline is wearing her new three-piece playsuit, and if she should get cool, there is a cardigan, slacks, and blouse. They have a "simply grand" picnic in the woods beside the river.

ONE FINE MORNING: It is marketing day for Cook, and she promised to take Lucy along. The chauffeur arrives with the car, and Lucy is ready with Madeline dressed in a flowered skirt and lacy blouse. The next time Madeline goes to market, she will wear the other dress shown on this brochure page.

SINGING IN THE RAIN: Mother reminds Lucy not to oversleep because today was her day to take baskets to the Orphans Home. She dressed Madeline in another new outfit – a raincoat and hat over her dotted swiss pinafore dress.

WEDDING DAY: Lucy and her friend, Carol, are bridesmaids. Lucy asks Mother to have a dress made for Madeline just like hers. While having a bridemaid's gown made for Madeline, Lucy's mother also had a ballgown made. Pictures of both appear on this page, and the cost of the extra packaged outfits are $12.95 each. (Remember, this was 1952 and that was a week's rent.)

AFTERNOON AT THE BEACH: Lucy spends time with her friend, Carol, at the seashore and takes Madeline along who is dressed in suitable beach wear. For evenings, Madeline always dressed in a "sweet summer frock." Pictures of the outfits are on the page.

TELEVISION UNTIL EIGHT: Daddy was away so Lucy and her mother, along with Madeline, are in the library and have been served supper in front of the fire. Then as the clock in the hall strikes eight, Mother takes Lucy and Madeline up the long stairs to put them to bed. This clothes description ends with, "It has been a wonderful summer for a doll named Madeline and for Lucy who loves her."

This booklet also includes July 4th, Trip to the City, and Lucy Goes Shopping. All of these pages show pictures of clothes available for the doll.

Madame Bea Alexander was a designer of clothes and a businesswoman who had the personality it took to survive in the harsh business world of the 1930s and 1940s. She was exceptional considering the doll and toy fields were dominated by men. Madame's husband, best friends, and even her child would encourage her to "get out of the rat race" from time to time, but that would always spur her on to greater things.

It must be remembered the doll themselves meant little except figures in the cost columns. It was the *clothes* that made the doll! To Madame Alexander, the doll formula was 90% clothes, 5% hair, and 5% doll.

Madame loved to make adult dolls because they were wonderful to design for and easier to dress. She had adult dolls made of composition and hard plastic.

By enjoying her company, much was learned from this lady through causal conversation. One had to laugh at the hits and misses that happened daily in such a business. On one such occasion, the subject of high heels came up after observing an elderly lady wearing spike heels attempt to get into a car.

"Do you know Cissy?" asked Madame as if Cissy was a real person. I nodded. "She was a first with high heel feet, and I asked for them to be designed that way from our maker. Well, she was around for awhile, and we kept receiving a few letters that her long stockings would slip down. They had not done this on the flat-footed dolls. Later, we received letters after we introduced Cissette, Cissy's little sister, so I was disturbed." At such a mild description of her aggravation, I turned to face her and saw the smile on her face turn to a deep frown. She continued, "The answer came to me at dinner one evening, so the next morning I had an order sent in for extra long stockings and had a seamstress split a pair and sew them together. It worked. Cissy was about to be discontinued, but I used those stocking hose on other dolls. One day a man came to my office and asked me if he could use that idea. I said 'Of course, why not.' Well, my dear, there it is. I invented *pantyhose* and *leotards* and had no idea I had as I was just interested in pleasing all those (pause) little girls out there." I'm certain the pause was the mental word "retailers," but was replaced by the word she spoke.

Many collectors feel the Madame Alexander Doll Company should have made the Shirley Temple dolls, but there was a reason they didn't. Madame Alexander explained to it to me as well as to reporter John Platero, who wrote for *The Evening News* of Harrisburg, PA. In an article for his "Lifestyles" column, dated October 31, 1978, he quoted her as saying: "I always thought Shirley Temple was extremely talented, but about the time she became a child star, I had been quoted in a newspaper interview that I disapproved of commercializing on a child's efforts. Because I couldn't go against what I had said, I did not make the doll." She admitted it hurt her company financially at the time, but problems were soon diminished when she was given permission by the Canadian government to make the Dionne Quints after visiting the children in person.

(For a more information about Madame Alexander, locate the following books by Pat Smith: *Madame Alexander Dolls, Volumes 1 and 2*; *The World of Alexanderkins,* and *The Encyclopedia of Madame Alexander Dolls.* Also Madame Alexander dolls will be found in *Modern Collector Dolls, Volumes 1–7.* They can be purchased through Collector Books or found in your local library.)

DEDICATION: TO THE MEMORY OF WENDY ANN BIRNBAWM

FROM THE THOUGHTS OF A LOVING GRAND-MOTHER:

Wendy Ann was a delightful child, full of fun and laughter. She had a great capacity for friendship and was always a leader in her group. Everyone loved her. When vacations came along she would bring some students to her home and do everything to make them enjoy that vacation.

From an early age she showed great musical talent. When listening to music she was able to return home and remember the score. She had perfect pitch and played the piano at the age of five. At age ten she played in a concert and the passion and the emotion she played from a piece of Spanish music brought tears and applause from the audience. To me it looked as if the piano lifted from the floor.

She attended Bennington College and changed from the arts, she chose to help the less fortunate and planned a career of Social Work.

Wendy passed away at 21 of an Embolism caused by the Asiatic Flu, a terrible accident, as one in a million survived.

Her parakeet,"Pretty Boy" was taken care of fully by Wendy Ann. He died at age fourteen which many said was unheard of. He brought a happy reminder of the beautiful girl that lived with us so short a time. When Wendy Ann passed away I prayed that I should die because it was so painful. My family and my many friends were so patient and considerate and understanding, which gave me the courage to go on. I now want to thank all my sincere doll collectors for the many beautiful letters and quotations from the poets, who had the bitter experience of losing one as I did, whom I loved so much.

Madame Alexander

This letter from Madame Alexander is printed with the permission of her grandson, Mr. William (Bill) Birnbawn.

20" OLD FASHIONED GIRL (Betty), #362,678–1936. Based on book of the same name by Louisa Mae Alcott. Made of all composition with closed mouth and tin sleep eyes. (Eyes are without celluloid overlay used in earlier years that turned a yellowish color.) A sweet doll that is all original. $700.00. *Courtesy Kris Lundquist.*

11" DIONNE QUINT toddler ANNETTE from 1937 to 1938. Made of all composition with sleep eyes. All original. $350.00 up. *Courtesy Gloria Anderson.*

Left: 11" RUMBERA made 1938 to 1943. Right: 11" SCARLETT made 1938 to 1942. Both are all composition and original. Both use the WENDY ANN doll. SCARLETT is from 1938, before the movie. Note gold label on her skirt. RUMBERA - $385.00; SCARLETT - $600.00 up. *Courtesy Sally Bethschieder.*

15" all composition CARMEN made from 1937 to 1940. Uses the WENDY ANN doll with sleep eyes. Earrings are attached to headpiece. All original and in near mint condition. $475.00. *Courtesy Carmen Holshoe.*

18" all composition PRINCESS ELIZABETH made in 1937 to 1941. Has sleep eyes and human hair wig. Crown is metal. All original, fully marked, and tagged. $700.00 up. *Courtesy Jeannie Nespoli.*

19" all composition McGUFFEY ANA that uses the PRINCESS ELIZABETH marked mold. This is a rare outfit and is tagged "McGuffey Ana." Made in 1937 to 1943. $750.00 up. *Courtesy Jeannie Nespoli.*

18" all composition SONJA HENIE BRIDE from 1940 with sleep eyes and open mouth. All original dress with extra long veil that drapes over her arm. $950.00. *Courtesy Jeannie Nespoli.*

18" all composition SONJA HENIE from 1941. All original. $950.00. *Courtesy Jeannie Nespoli.*

14" hard plastic PRINCESS MARGARET ROSE from 1950. Has beautiful face color. All original and tagged. In mint condition - $850.00. *Courtesy Susan Girardot.*

14" strung MARGARET from in the early 1950s dressed in separate boxed outfit made of taffeta. Came in 15", 18", and 23" sizes. Outfit shown in regular brochures and for 18" MADELINE. Colors included green/white and blue/white. $400.00. *Courtesy June Schutlz.*

14" MARGARET from 1952 dressed in all original tagged outfit and shoes that were sold separately in garment bag. Outfit also came in 18" size and in various pastel colors. $465.00. *Courtesy June Schultz.*

18" hard plastic doll with MARGARET face. Has heavy mohair wig and a crisp pink dress (#345F $4.95 retail). This is one of the dresses made for the hard plastic MADELINE doll, 1950–1953, and is shown in her brochure. $465.00 up. *Courtesy Jeannie Nespoli.*

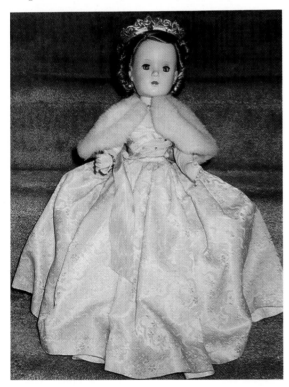

17" all hard plastic QUEEN from the Glamour Girl series of 1953. She is a MARGARET face doll with saran wig and sleep eyes. All original. $700.00 up.

Courtesy Jeannie Nespoli.

18" hard plastic ballerina with MARGARET face. Has sleep eyes and lavender tutu with rhinestone bodice. She is a walker doll, and her head turns from side to side as her legs move. From 1950. $625.00. *Courtesy Jeannie Nespoli.*

18" MAGGIE with floss hair. Wearing separate boxed outfit, #214-1952, made of organdy and dotted swiss. (Also came in 15", 18", and 23" sizes.) Outfit came in Copenhagen blue with red dots and sky blue with pink dots. $600.00. *Courtesy June Schultz.*

15" MAGGIE WALKER sold through FAO Schwarz in 1952. She is wearing boxed outfit #275 that was sold separately. (See variation of skirt in *Modern Collector's Dolls Volume 5,* pg. 24.) Also came in 18" and 23" sizes. $425.00 up. *Courtesy June Schultz.*

14" hard plastic MAGGIE SKATER with large round sleep eyes. She is a walker and her head turns as legs are moved. All original except for socks. Tam should be positioned lower to one side of head. Made 1949–1953. $500.00 up. *Courtesy Jeannie Nespoli.*

14" hard plastic KATHY SKATER of 1951. All original including purse which is the same color and material as skates. In mint condition. $550.00 up. *Courtesy Susan Girardot.*

20" CISSY from the mid 1950s. Made of all hard plastic with vinyl arms jointed at the elbows. Has high heel feet. All original. $350.00 up. *Courtesy Jeannie Nespoli.*

"DREAMS COME TRUE" CISSY as Queen Elizabeth II dressed in white brocade gown. All original. (Note necklace of pearls with drop goldtone beads. Made in 1955. $950.00. *Courtesy Jeannie Nespoli.*

10½" CISSETTE, #755-1962, with jointed knees. The 1963 version has three rows of lace around skirt and is #755. $285.00.

Group of four 10" CISSETTES in street dresses. All are original except second from left has replaced shoes. Each - $265.00. *Courtesy Sally Bethschieder.*

10" CISSETTES used as various dolls. The two on the left are MARGOT dolls with elaborate hairdos. Next to them is CISSETTE as herself, dressed in a sunsuit. At the far right is CISSETTE as BEAUTY QUEEN. All are original. Each - $265.00. *Courtesy Sally Bethschieder.*

10" BABBETTE Portrette of 1988 (Cissette). $75.00.

10" SAILORETTE Portrette of 1988 (Cissette). $75.00.

10" CLAUDETTE Portrette of 1988 (Cissette). $75.00.

This is the very first RED RIDING HOOD and is very rare, especially in this mint condition. She is a straight leg walker, and her cape folds under her arms and is stitched down. $450.00 up. *Courtesy Margaret Mandel.*

8" QUIZ-KIN has lever in her back to make head nod "yes" or "no." She is a straight leg non-walker made of all hard plastic. Original. Made 1953–1954. $575.00. *Courtesy Kris Lundquist.*

8" SCOUTING is from the Americana Series and was made in 1991 and 1992 only. $45.00 up. *Courtesy Gloria Woods.*

8" EASTER BUNNY made for Child at Heart Doll Shoppe of Dallas in 1991. Special stand made and designed by Ann Rast. $300.00 up.

8" OLIVER TWIST is part of the Storybook Series and was only made in 1992. Stand is by A.C.T. Designs. $45.00 up.

8" *Gone With The Wind* dolls from recent years. They include SCARLETT, RHETT, MELAINE, PRISSY, MAMMY, BELLE WATLING, BONNIE BLUE, ASHLEY, and MR. AND MRS. O'HARA. Each - $55.00 up. *Courtesy Carmen Holshoe.*

8" BONNIE BLUE from the Scarlett Series. Made from 1990 to 1992. $55.00. *Courtesy Roger Jones.*

8" SAK'S OWN CHRISTMAS CAROL made in 1993. Special stand by A.C.T. Designs. Without stand - $75.00 up.

8" mid-year introduction dolls, ROMERO and JULIET, were made in 1994 only. Stand designed and made by Ann Rast. Without stand - $125.00 each.

8" CAROLINE'S STORYBOOK TRUNK AND WARDROBE made exclusively for Neiman-Marcus in 1994. $265.00 up.

SECRET GARDEN is one of the finest exclusives created. Made for FAO Schwarz in 1994. She comes in a metal trunk and has two other fine quality outfits. $300.00.

WENDY STARTS HER COLLECTION is an exclusive doll made for Jacobson's in 1994. Limited to 2,400 dolls. $80.00.

WENDY'S FAVORITE PASTIME is an adorable doll made exclusively for Disney in 1994. She carries her hula hoop and has a special hairdo. $75.00.

8" SETTING SAIL FOR SUMMER (Wendy Ann) was created specially for the 1994 Madame Alexander Doll Club Premiere. $135.00.

12" vinyl LITTLE SHAVER with painted features was made from 1963 to 1965. All original, autographed by Madame Alexander. $275.00. *Courtesy Floyd & Gracie James.*

18" cloth and vinyl ALLISON was made from 1990 to 1991 only. $95.00.

24" BONNIE, the 1961 or 1962 winner of the Miss America crown. Made by Allied-Grand Doll Mfg. Inc., stock number #3955. If it has a wrist tag, it will state: "An Allied Quality Doll/Bonnie." Original - $60.00. *Courtesy Kathy Tvrdik.*

⇜ American Character ⇝

American Character began their business using the mark ACEEDEECEE (a phoneticism of the company initials.) The mark was used for a very short time, then it changed to PETITE. In the 1930s, this firm changed its name to American Character Doll Company and changed it again in 1960 to American Doll and Toy Company.

American Character was the first to use rooted hair by making a rubber cap (later a vinyl cap) and rooting the hair into it like a wig. Part of the hard plastic head was cut out, allowing the rubber or vinyl wig cap to be glued onto the head. This process gave the head a correct dimensional look. The doll hair used was washable and combable. This method was covered by patent number 2,675,644.

Sweet Sue Sophisticate and Toni were high heeled, grown-up versions of Sweet Sue. Toni dolls were made to promote Gillette's line of Toni cosmetics and hair products. Each doll came with play wave kits that allowed the child to change their doll's hair to six different styles. These dolls came in sizes 10½", 14", 20", 25". The hard plastic/vinyl versions came in 30–33" size. Some of the most beautiful clothes ever designed for *any* dolls were made by American Character for these two dolls.

Other famous dolls by American Character were Betsy McCall, Tressy (a fashion doll with grow hair), and Toodles.

The most popular doll made by American Character was Sweet Sue. The first attempts to make hard plastics dolls occurred in late 1948. The actual process was not finalized until 1949 when Kodac came up with the injection moulding system for doll companies.

It must be remembered that not all the doll companies had the money, expertise, or room for the extremely large vats, rollers, conveyor belts, multi-hangers, and high density air ejection systems needed for doll production. There is no question that three main doll manufacturers – Alexander, American Character, and Arranbee – used a common mould maker for doll parts. The parts were shipped to their companies where assembly and marketing took place. The heads for these three companies were designed by Bernard Lipfert, and in the case of American Character, the clothes were designed by Beatrice Sandler Rose. Likewise, other leading clothing designers produced doll clothes and one such main designer was Mollye Goldman of Mollye Internationals.

In 1957, American Character had Agop Agapoli design a prototype that was submitted to McCall Corp. This lead to the birth of the popular 7½–8" Betsy McCall. This all hard plastic doll had hundreds of costumes available for her as well as furniture and accessories.

In 1958, the Gillette Company, who owned the Toni Company, allowed American Character to produce Toni dolls which used the Sweet Sue Sophisticate dolls. Now as then, these dolls are greatly loved by their owners. The vinyl used for these dolls was some of the finest available. Since Agop Agapoli also designed the heads for these dolls, they have his characteristic large, round eyes.

By 1963, American Character had to try something to counteract Barbie and introduced a more "hometown" style girl – Tressy, a fashion doll with the unique feature of growing hair. Outfits for the doll were sold separately, but the clothing quality was less than her predecessors'. This is part of the reason why these dolls were not on the market for long.

The company had to produce dolls at a lower price to survive, and Tressy and her clothes were made in the East. This did not work well, and in an effort to save the company, Herbert Brock and his son, Jacob, started importing dolls from Europe under their name. This occurred in the mid-1960s, and because the idea was before its time, it failed. The company went out of business in 1967. Much of the usable equipment was purchased by Ideal Doll & Toy Company, including the patent for the grow hair feature. Ideal eventually used this feature on Crissy and her friends in the 1970s.

15" SWEET SUE WALKER from 1955. Made of all hard plastic with saran wig. All original. (22" version can be seen in *Modern Collector's Dolls, Volume 1*, pg. 77. 14" doll is in *Modern Collector's Dolls, Volume 5*, pg. 46, but skirt has six rows of net.) $265.00 up. *Courtesy Karen Stephenson.*

18" SWEET SUE in evening gown with braid coronet over top of head. Has curlers in hat box on arm. All original, mint condition. $325.00 up.

Early 18" SWEET SUE dressed in original gown with lace bodice and ruffle/lace at hip. This is fashion treatment favored American Character. $325.00 up.

Courtesy June Schultz.

18" SWEET SUE PROM DATE from 1954. All original hard plastic walker with sleep eyes and glued-on wig. $325.00 up. *Courtesy June Schultz.*

18" SWEET SUE BRIDE from 1955. Made of hard plastic with jointed knees. Vinyl arms are jointed at elbows. (Also in *Modern Collector's Dolls, Volume 1*, pg. 31.) Original - $325.00 up.

20" SWEET SUE WALKER made of all hard plastic. Head turns from side to side as she walks. All original. $350.00 up.

24" all hard plastic SWEET SUE WALKER dressed in original gown. Marked "Amer. Char." on head. $375.00 up. *Courtesy Glorya Woods.*

30" hard plastic SWEET SUE BRIDESMAID with vinyl arms. She is a walker. Head turns as she walks. All original, mint condition. $425.00 up. *Courtesy Marjoie Uhl.*

30" SWEET SUE COTILLION from 1955. All hard plastic walker. Also came in yellow and pink. Original and in mint condition. $450.00 up. *Courtesy Evelyn Samec.*

28" SWEET SUE that is an all hard plastic walker. All original with wrist tag. In this condition - $450.00.
Courtesy Marjorie Uhl.

20" ANNIE OAKLEY is an all hard plastic walker with flat feet. Her name is stitched on oilcloth type skirt. Satin blouse has oilcloth cuffs. Hat has cut edges to form fringe. This doll was made in 1956. (The 1955 version was blonde with twin ponytails and curled under bangs.) All original, mint condition. $500.00 up. *Courtesy Barbara Male.*

Very cute 15" SWEET SUE with original skirt, blouse, and jacket. She most likely had a hat. Shoes and hair ribbon are replaced. Made of all hard plastic. $350.00 up.

18" all hard plastic SWEET SUE with vinyl arms, inset wig, and flat feet. She is a walker with jointed knees and elbows. Has cotton blouse, felt skirt, cap, and purse with wrist tie. $400.00 up. *Courtesy Elizabeth Montesano.*

21" all hard plastic SWEET SUE has felt skirt, hat, and purse. Satin slip is made to show under skirt. $400.00 up.

14" and 17" SWEET SUE dolls wearing original outfits. These all hard plastic walkers are the childhood dolls of owner Pat Clark Pratt. 14" - $400.00. 17" - $650.00.

18" SWEET SUE with inset saran wig and sleep eyes. All hard plastic walker with flat feet. All original except shoes and socks. $250.00 up. *Courtesy Jeannie Nespoli.*

20" all hard plastic SWEET SUE made in early 1950s. All original and childhood doll of owner. $300.00 up.

Courtesy Pat Pratt.

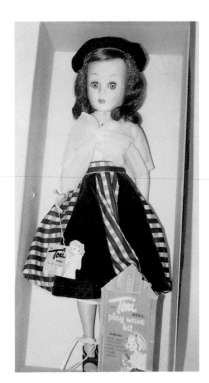

20" all hard plastic SWEET SUE from 1950s. Has sleep eyes and saran wig rooted into vinyl cap. Cap fits cut out area of head. In mint condition and shown with original box. Mint in box - $450.00 up. Near mint condition - $325.00.

Very rare 20" TONI made by American Character. Has rare hairdo with deep side part. All original in original box with wave kit. $600.00 up. *Courtesy Susan Girardot.*

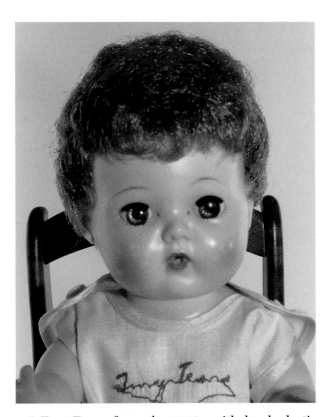

12" TEENY TINY TEARS from the 1960s. All vinyl and dressed in outfit from 1963 McCall's pattern. $45.00.

Courtesy Pat Graff.

11" TINY TEARS from the 1950s with hard plastic head and vinyl body. All original. Marked "Pat. No. 2675644." Mint condition - $185.00. Played with - $100.00. *Courtesy Glorya Woods.*

All three sizes of AMERICAN BEAUTY TONI by American Character. All are made of vinyl and original. 10½" - $200.00 up. 14" - $285.00 up. 21" - $375.00 up. *Courtesy Charmaine Shields.*

Two WHIMSIE dolls that are getting a bath. Shows body construction quite well. Vinyl body and limbs are made in one piece. Also has vinyl head. On left is FRIAR and the one with molded closed eyes is BESSIE. Dressed - $95.00 each. *Courtesy Pat Graff.*

Among the WHIMSIES are two girls that are exactly the same except for hair color. The blonde haired girl is DIXIE THE PIXIE. The other with pink hair is POLLY THE LOLLY. Both wear the same outfit and hold a lollipop. Each - $95.00.

17" ORPHAN ANNIE with yarn hair, molded "v" style chin, cloth body, and stockinette head and arms. Shoes and socks are sewn onto legs. Eyes are painted upward. Tagged "Applause 1962 Columbia Pictures Ind. Inc. 1962 Tribune Company Syn, Inc. $85.00.

15½" all soft sculpture doll, THE EXECUTIVE, with mohair wig and brows. Marketed by Applause in 1986. $45.00. *Courtesy Pat Graff.*

On the left and right are two GUPPY dolls. In the center is BUBBA. All are made from vinyl doll kits produced by Apple Valley Doll Works. Each - $85.00. *Courtesy Theo Lindley.*

13" PRINCESS BETTY ROSE uses a reduced version of the DEBU-TEEN head on an all composition body. Has tin sleep eyes and mohair wig in original set. Her purse matches the jacket. Marked "R & B." All original, ca. 1935. $200.00 up. *Courtesy Kris Lundquist.*

14" NANETTE BRIDE made of hard plastic. All original in satin wedding gown, hooped petticoat, and long veil. $275.00. *Courtesy Patricia Wood.*

15" NANETTE is an "R&B" marked walker made of hard plastic. Wears ornate metal crown set with rhinestones. Detailed taffeta gown is accented with pearl shoulder straps, rhinestone clip, and flower and ribbon trim at waist. Has wired hoop skirt under gown. Shown in Orman's 1953 fall catalog as QUEEN AT BALL. (1953 was the year of Queen Elizabeth's coronation.) $425.00 up. *Courtesy Elizabeth Montesano.*

Cute 13" NANETTE BRIDE made of all hard plastic. Dates from 1953. Original and mint in her box. $165.00. *Courtesy Anita Pacey.*

20" NANETTE with beautiful gold gown trimmed in fur. Has ornate floss hairdo. Made of all hard plastic. A very special Arranbee doll. $375.00 up. *Courtesy Marjorie Uhl.*

21" NANETTE BRIDE of 1950. Made of all hard plastic and original. $375.00 up. *Courtesy Marjorie Uhl.*

21" NANETTE is an all hard plastic walker whose head turns from side to side. Her hair is very soft, but not mohair. All original. $175.00. *Courtesy Pat Graff.*

We know, we know, the hat is ridiculous, but the doll is great! 21" NANCY LEE or NANCY JEAN is made of all hard plastic. The originality of her clothes and accessories are questionable. (The hat remained on due to a three-year old's insistance.) $465.00 up.

10" MISS COTY from 1957 is made of all rigid vinyl with rooted hair, sleep eyes, and high heel feet. Early versions of this doll had hard plastic bodies with vinyl heads. All original and marked "Ⓟ." $125.00.

Courtesy Marie Ernst.

10½" MISS COTY is all vinyl with jointed waist and high heel feet. Has rooted hair and sleep eyes. All original. $150.00 up. *Courtesy Marie Ernst.*

10" LITTLEST ANGEL dolls made by Arranbee. They are all hard plastic walkers with jointed knees, sleep eyes, and glued-on wigs. All are wearing original clothes. Each - $95.00 up. *Courtesy Helena Street.*

14" KELLY dressed as #0009 "OLD FASHIONED GIRL." Made by Associated Dollmakers, Inc. in 1985 and designed by Yolando Bello. $90.00. *Courtesy Pat Graff.*

14" KIMBERLY dressed as #0008 "PARTY FINERY." Made by Associated Dollmakers, Inc. in 1985 and designed by Yolando Bello. $90.00. *Courtesy Pat Graff.*

16" official GIRL SCOUT dolls sold through Avon with a retail price of $40.00 each in 1995. Both are made of vinyl with cloth torsos. They should become collector's classics on the secondary market. $40.00 **up.** *Courtesy Susan Girardot.*

⚍ Barbie®⚍

The big question about Barbie doll is "How long will it last?" The question covers the rising prices of the doll and consumer demand. Will Mattel's practices be like Avon, Cabbage Patch, Madame Alexander, and so many other "high flyer" companies who have gone under. The foremost problem is overproduction. There is just so much to keep up with that it has overwhelmed the market. Mattel has recognized the "series" idea of marketing, as has Madame Alexander Doll Company. If a collector starts a series, they are generally going to continue and purchase the remainder of the collection. There has been some very far reaching "characters" appear in these series.

Like Alexander Doll Company, Mattel is putting out too many new dolls each year, and it is difficult for the average collector to keep up with them all. Also, both doll companies have found the "exclusive" doll market. Although Alexander has dramatically slowed its exclusives (although new owners may differ with this), Mattel has added more and more exclusives on the market.

Time will tell how long Mattel can continue its pace with their Barbie dolls. Speaking of time, any collector knows that in 200, even 500 years from now, any doll made after 1985 can be found either in *mint in box* (MIB) or *never removed from the box* (NRFB) condition. This applies especially to Barbie dolls. Hopefully, those collecting Barbie dolls love the doll and are not buying her strictly as an investment.

The word *investment* also raises the question, "How do prices happen?" Doll prices in the past few years have generally been set by dealers. Most mass purchases from a retailer are from dealers who know the demands and prices of their particular area. Often dolls will pass from dealer to dealer with the prices increasing with each step.

One interesting note about the Barbie doll is that it was first made in Japan and other Far East countries. Since the first dolls were made in Japan, the eyes are painted to the side. It is impossible to get a doll made in the Orient to look you in the eye. That goes for old and new souvenir dolls who have no pupils or have eyes that will not focus straight ahead. The reason is based on the Japanese belief that if a doll looks you straight in the eyes, it can take your soul. There is a lot of interesting history surrounding dolls in the Orient and the important part they play within their culture.

In 1991, this porcelain SOPHISTICATED LADY BARBIE doll was a limited edition that sold for $198.00. Now - $275.00 up. *Courtesy Mattel, Inc.*

Left to right: Brunette bubble cut BARBIE doll, mint in box. FASHION QUEEN BARBIE doll with wigs in mint condition. Mint in box #4 blonde BARBIE doll. In rear: Blonde bubble cut BARBIE doll with pale lips. Brunette bubble cut - $325.00. FASHION QUEEN - $500.00. #4 BARBIE doll - $275.00. Blonde bubble cut - $100.00.

Courtesy Turn of Century Antiques.

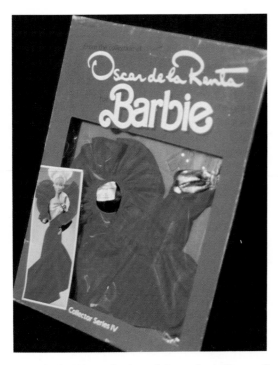

Two Oscar de la Renta designed, boxed outfits made exclusively for Barbie doll. Each - $60.00. *Courtesy Phyllis Kates.*

7" HONG KONG LILLI has Japan sticker on back of skirt. All original. $75.00 up. *Courtesy Susan Girardot.*

(See information about the LILLI dolls in *Modern Collector Dolls, Volume 7,* page 60. This also includes information on the HONG KONG LILLI.)

11½" German LILLI was made before BARBIE doll. She was imported and sold in some large department stores. All original in plastic circular display box with name on side of stand base. Blonde is shown but also came with brunette inset wigs. Rare in box (comparable to #1 Barbie.) Value unknown. *Courtesy Susan Girardot.*

HAPPY BIRTHDAY BARBIE doll dressed in a celebration gown! Made in 1990. $40.00. *Courtesy Kathy Tvrdik.*

SUMMIT BARBIE doll from 1990. $45.00. *Courtesy Kathy Tvrdik.*

1990 limited edition 30TH ANNIVERSARY BARBIE doll. Made in China. $100.00. *Courtesy Kathy Tvrdik.*

A beautiful BARBIE doll called STERLING WISHES was made as a limited edition for Spiegel's mail order in 1991. $95.00. *Courtesy Kathy Tvrdik.*

Limited edition HOLIDAY BARBIE doll from 1991.
Dressed in green velvet. Made in China. $85.00. *Courtesy
Kathy Tvrdik.*

HOLIDAY HOSTESS BARBIE doll from 1993. $20.00. *Courtesy
Marie Ernst.*

BARBIE FOR PRESIDENT gift set was made as a limited edition for Toys "R" Us in 1991. Back of box
has what appears to be the Presidential Seal on it. $30.00. *Courtesy Gloria Anderson.*

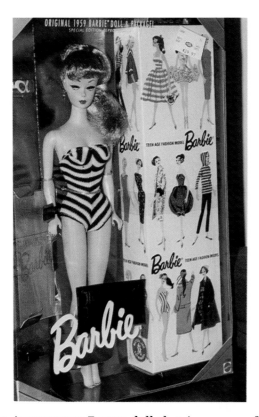

35TH ANNIVERSARY BARBIE doll that is a copy of the first 1959 doll and box. She even has the wrist tag. These can not be sold as old because the material they are made from is different and the hair has a different texture. $80.00. *Courtesy Gloria Anderson.*

TROLL BARBIE doll with large troll earrings, printed troll outfit, and different colored hairpieces. $25.00. *Courtesy Gloria Anderson.*

Special edition BARBIE doll from Kraft Treasures. She has "Kraft" on her hat and "Cheeasaurus Rex" on the bodice along with Kraft and BARBIE logos. Her tote bag is marked "Kraft Treasures." Made in 1992 and manufactured in China. The Linda Shelton family ate a lot of macaroni & cheese to get this doll! $30.00. *Courtesy the author.*

AUSTRALIAN BARBIE doll made in 1993. $25.00. *Courtesy Marie Ernst.*

FLAPPER BARBIE doll from the Great Eras Series of 1993. $52.00. *Courtesy Marie Ernst.*

SPOTS 'N DOTS BARBIE and TERESA dolls were made as a limited edition for Toys "R" Us in 1993. Each - $30.00. *Courtesy Marie Ernst.*

EASTER FUN BARBIE doll was a supermarket special in 1993. Has Easter egg earrings, print dress, and instructions for making Easter eggs. Was hard to find in some parts of the country. $45.00. *Courtesy Beth Summers.*

BENEFIT BALL BARBIE doll was a limited edition doll designed by Carol Spencer in 1992. $40.00. *Courtesy Phyllis Kates.*

GOLDEN JUBILEE BARBIE doll from 1994 is considered by most collectors as the most beautiful BARBIE doll ever made. $1,200.00. *Courtesy Turn of Century Antiques.*

VICTORIAN ELEGANCE BARBIE doll was made as a special for Hallmark in 1994. $20.00. *Courtesy Gloria Anderson.*

DISNEY FUN BARBIE dolls were made exclusively for Disneyland and Disney World in 1993. Each - $30.00. *Courtesy Gloria Anderson.*

Betsy McCall

All of the Betsy McCall dolls are highly collectible because they are very recognizable. Often they are associated with childhood memories of the collector — either the doll itself or the paper dolls found in McCall's magazine.

Several years ago, a book was compiled on McCall dolls, but the author was told by the McCall Corporation that they were doing their own book on the subject. So far, none has been published. Perhaps one will appear in the near future.

This author cautions collectors about the prices that will be demanded for Betsy McCall dolls after the company does issue their own price guide. This same "creating a market" has been done by many companies, and it often spells disaster for the collector. Those that set their own collectible prices are Annalee, Hallmark, Dept. 56, and soon to be Daddy Long Legs. More are sure to follow. So collectors, just be careful out there!

(For more information on sizes and makers of Betsy McCall dolls, please see *Modern Collector Dolls, Volume 6,* pg. 41.)

22" BETSY McCALL with multi-jointed body, including ankles, wrists, and waist. Has brown eyes and original clothes. Shoes and socks have been replaced. (Could she also be a TERRY TWIST by Ideal with this hairdo?) $300.00 up. *Courtesy Pat Graff.*

Both of these 8" BETSY McCALL dolls are made of hard plastic with extra joints at the knees. Their original dresses are styled the same, but the material colors are different. Both are marked "1958 McCall." Each - $225.00. *Courtesy Glorya Woods.*

A very beautiful 8" Betsy McCall in a tiered wedding gown with ruffles. She is all original and in mint condition. $245.00. *Courtesy Turn of Century Antiques.*

8" Betsy McCall skater and ballerina. Both are all original. (Photo has been shown previously in black & white, but needs to be seen in color to fully appreciate the outfits.) Each - $245.00.

14" vinyl and 8" hard plastic Betsy McCall dolls made by American Character and dressed in "Playtime #2." 14" - $285.00; 8" - $185.00. *Courtesy Peggy Pergande.*

14" Betsy McCall made of all vinyl with a rather square face and large round eyes. Marked "McCall/ 1958." All original and in mint condition. $450.00. *Courtesy Susan Girardot.*

14" BETSY McCALL in original trunk with wardrobe. All is in mint, unplayed with condition. Doll only - $285.00. With wardrobe - $500.00.

Three sizes of BETSY McCALL dolls. The 20" and 14" ones are made of vinyl. The 8" doll in made of all hard plastic. The 20" doll has a knee length dress and flirty eyes that move from side to side. 20" - $325.00 up. 14" - $285.00 up. 8" - $245.00 up.

17" GOLDILOCKS made of plastic and vinyl with sleep eyes, closed smiling mouth, and original clothes. The apron has her name imprinted on it. Head is marked "Brookglad" and has "1756-G2" on back. The three bears came with the doll. Surely they are Steiff ZOTZY bears (1957–1971) but lack button or tag. Yet they have vertically stitched yarn noses and the lightened chest plate of Steiff. (Hermann also made this style of bears.) Set - $225.00. (Doll also appears in *Modern Collector Dolls, Volume 5*, pg. 61.)
Courtesy The Doll Cradle.

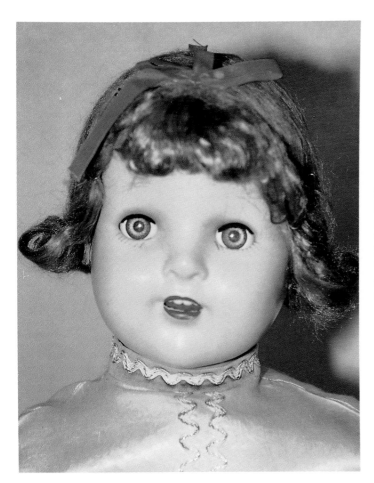

28" DADDY'S QUEEN with composition head, cloth body, and latex limbs. She has sleep eyes/lashes and painted lower lashes. Wears original dress with dark blue skirt. Head marked "APEX." Doll tagged "Daddy's Queen" and on the reverse, "Brown & Richie, Ltd." with three symbols of a crown, a lion inside a shield, and "BR" inside a square. In mint condition - $60.00.

⌒ Cabbage Patch Kids ⌒

Original Appalachian Artworks of Cleveland, Georgia, under the supervision of Xavier Roberts, has made soft-sculptured original Little People® and Cabbage Patch Kids® since 1978, and has licensed the manufacture of vinyl-headed Cabbage Patch Kids since 1983. The Kids are loved for their whimsy and "one-of-a-kind" individuality.

Original Appalachian Artworks (P.O. Box 714, Cleveland, GA 30528) provides information on new original editions in their bi-monthly newsletter, "Limited Edition," published for members of their Collector's Club. A monthly newsletter, primarily for collectors of the mass-market Cabbage Patch Kids, is available from Ann Wilhite, 610 W. 17th, Fremont, NE 68025. "The Cabbage Connection" includes in-depth articles, collector profiles, news updates, and lists of Kids for sale or trade. Ann's publication was the source for doll information and values in this section.

Soft-sculptured Originals: Little People, 1978–1982, and Cabbage Patch Kids since 1983. Babies before 1981 are hand-signed by Xavier Roberts. Edition is determined by birth certificate or name tag; for verification, contact O.A.A.'s customer service department.

1978	"Helen" Blue	$3,500.00 up
1978	"A" Blue	$3,900.00 up
1978–79	"B" Red	$2,400.00 up
1979	"C" Burgundy	$1,500.00 up
1979	"D" Purple	$900.00 up
1979–80	"E" Bronze	$500.00 up
1983	Oriental set	$750.00 up
1983	American Indian set	$750.00 up
1983	Champagne Madeira and Andre set (5th Anniversary)	$700.00 up

Cabbage Patch Kids® with vinyl heads and soft-sculptured bodies, ©O.A.A., 1978, 1982, with facsimile "Xavier Roberts" signature on left buttocks, have been manufactured for U.S. distribution by Coleco, 1983–1989; Hasbro, 1989–1994; and Mattel since 1995. Foreign manufacturers, 1983–1985, were Jesmar (Spain), Lili Ledy (Mexico), Triang-Pedigree (South Africa), and Tsukuda (Japan). Date of manufacture is determined by color of signature. Prices are for mint dolls with complete outfit, birth certificate, adoption papers, and accessories. Value is affected by the rarity of certain face molds, hair and eye combinations, skin color, and freckles, as well as by outfits and the circled letters on body tags.

Coleco 1985 Cabbage Patch Kids with highly desirable UT body tags. Back row, left to right: #1 face mold, red braids, blue eyes; #4 face mold, brown top ponytail, brown eyes; #4 tan poodle hair and ponytails. Front: #4 lemon ponytails, blue eyes; #2 face mold, red ponytails, green eyes. Each - $50.00 up. *Courtesy Ann Wilhite.*

Coleco, 1983 (black signature) . . . .$30.00 up
   Black freckled kids. $225.00–400.00
   Red fuzzy-haired boys . . . $175.00–400.00
   Brown fuzzy-haired boys . . $75.00–175.00
   Freckled girls or boys . . . . $60.00 up
Coleco, 1984 – 89 . . . .$25.00 up
Specialty lines are generally more collectible.
   World Travelers, 1985
     (blue signature) $40.00–75.00
   Twins, 1985–86 . . . . $60.00–125.00
   Astronauts, 1986
     (red signature) $50.00–100.00
   Baseball All-Stars, 1986 . . . . $45.00–75.00
   Circus Kids, 1986
     (clowns and ringmaster). . $50.00–75.00
   Cornsilks, 1986–87 . . . . . . $25.00–75.00
   Talking Kids, 1987. . . . . $100.00 up
   Designer Line Kids, 1989 (rose-red
     undated signature) $25.00–100.00
   "Popcorn" hair, 1986 . . . . . $30.00–125.00

Foreign manufacturers, 1983–85. Distributors include Ideal (England and France), Giocadipiu Giocadag (Italy), and Kaalitarhan Tenavat (Finland).
   Jesmar, Spain $30.00–150.00
   Tsukuda, Japan . . . .$30.00 up
     Specialty outfits (kimono, samuri,
      baseball) $60.00
     Wedding set $150.00–250.00
     Twins $150.00–200.00
   Triang-Pedigree, S. Africa . .$35.00–200.00
   Lili Ledy, Mexico $75.00–250.00

Hasbro, 1989 – 94 . . . .$20.00 up
   16" Kids $25.00–75.00
   Teeny Tiny Preemie Twins
     (Oriental and Hispanic sets) $50.00

Tsukuda 1985 girl (made in Japan) with hard-to-find lemon single braid and brown eyes. Wears baseball outfit. $100.00. *Courtesy Cindy Shaffer.*

Coleco 1985 WORLD TRAVELER from Holland. #5 single tooth face mold, lemon ponytails, blue eyes, OK body tag. Comes with flight bag, passport, airline ticket, and souvenir T-shirt. $60.00. *Courtesy Ann Wilhite.*

⌒ Cameo ⌒

Joseph Kallus helped design dolls for the George Borgfeldt Company when he was still an art student. At age 20, he went to work for one of Borgfeldt's firms and soon became the president of another. These were the Mutual Doll Company and K & K Company.

In late 1925, he started his own firm called "Cameo" and signed a contract with Rose O'Neill to make the Kewpies. Over the years, Cameo made many other collectible dolls, and the quality is among the best.

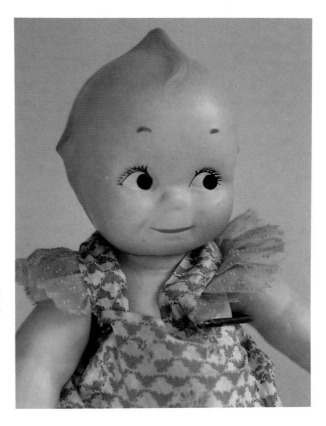

15" all composition KEWPIE shown in original romper suit from the 1940s. There were many variations of this romper suit. $295.00. *Courtesy Ken Bowers.*

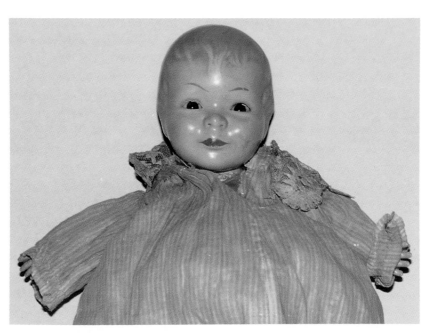

13" FLY-LO made by K & K Company when Joseph Kallus was designer/manager. Has a composition head, composition gauntlet hands, cloth body and limbs. $1,000.00 up. *Courtesy Ellen Dodge.* **(For photo of a very rare bisque version, see *Patricia Smith's Doll Values, Tenth Edition*, pg. 45.)**

Left: 13½" all celluloid KEWPIE with original sticker on stomach. Right: 13" all composition that has been redressed. Each - $295.00. *Courtesy Turn of Century Antiques.*

13" all composition KEWPIE with painted features. Jointed at neck, shoulder, and hips. All original from 1930s. $285.00. *Courtesy Carmen Holshoe.*

11" KEWPIE GAL made in 1974 when AMSCO had the rights to make KEWPIES. Hair is molded and has cloth ribbon. All original in box. Head marked "Cameo." $35.00. *Courtesy Glorya Woods.*

16" MISS PEEP used as BABY WENDY and marked so on box. Box makes into cradle. Doll is all stuffed vinyl with inset eyes and hinged joints. Sold through Montgomery Wards. Marked "Cameo." All original, in this condition - $65.00. *Courtesy Jeannie Mauldin.*

Left: 12" all celluloid carnival doll with original celluloid hat, real feathers, and floss skirt. Shoes, socks, and gold hair are painted on. Jointed at shoulders only. Made in Japan. $95.00. *Courtesy Kathy Tvrdik.*

Right: 15" chalk carnival figure from early to mid-1930s. Given as prizes at place such as Atlantic City, Coney Island, and Long Beach, California pier. $90.00. *Courtesy Kathy Tvrdik.*

16" painted chalk "smoker" doll. Note cigarette in her mouth. This carnival doll is from early to mid-1930s. $75.00.

8" plastic and vinyl L.A. Looks are made by Cititoy. All have painted features and rooted hair. These are rather inexpensive dolls, but cute. It will be fun in a few years to look at these dolls and remember the clothes and hairstyles of the early 1990s. Each - $12.00. *Courtesy Pat Graff.*

15" BECKY made by Cititoy in 1990. Has cloth body, vinyl head and hands, sleep eyes with hair lashes, and rooted hair. In mint condition. $15.00. *Courtesy Pat Graff.*

5½" GARDEN PRINCESS dolls made by Coleco in 1987. Their right hands are cupped to hold wand. Left: Platinum rooted hair, lavendar eyes. Center: Blonde hair, blue eyes. Right: Red hair, blue eyes. All are marked "Coleco/Made in China." Each - $9.00.

11" cloth doll from 1930s with pressed face mask, painted features, and oilcloth body. Has curly yarn hair with original bow. Dress and panties tagged "Made by Krueger." It must be noted that Mollye International purchased many sizes of this doll as well as one with eyes painted to the side from Krueger, so tags are very important. $135.00 up.

Courtesy Patricia Wood.

25" all printed cloth JOE MONTANA doll in his San Fransico 49ers #16 uniform. (He was #19 for the Kansas City Chiefs.) Made by Ace Novelty Co. $30.00.

10" CAROLE, the "dress me" doll of the late 1950s and early 1960s. Made of vinyl with swivel waist and high heel feet. Made by Commonwealth who also supplied a great many "blank" (unmarked) dolls to various companies who dressed and marketed them. Shoes came in packaging with her. $45.00 up. *Courtesy Marie Ernst.*

CAROLE made of all hard plastic with vinyl head, rooted hair, sleep eyes, and high heel feet. Earrings are pushed through the vinyl and into head. Made by Commonwealth in the mid-1950s. $10.00.

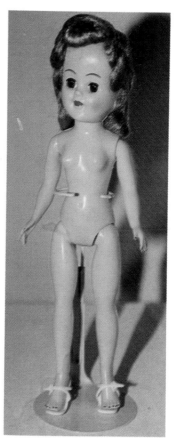

10" CAROLE, the "dress yourself" doll made by Commonwealth Plastics Corp. from 1959 to 1965. She is a walker with head that turns. She has sleep eyes and molded lashes. Doll and shoes came in plastic bag stapled to cardboard header. She was also made in a thin 8" size. $14.00.

≈ Composition Repair ≈

When a collector has a composition doll that needs repair, they must first determine just how much the doll means to them as repair is time consuming and demands many hours to complete just one doll.

Betty Barclift, who repairs composition dolls, said, "I know repair reduces the value, but they are, after all, only dolls meant to be loved, cherished, and played with. If others want to use them for investments, that's fine, but a lot of us just want to recapture lost, easier times, when we were young and more carefree."

Repair of composition is not as easy to decide upon as with antique bisque or china doll repair. The final line is what the owner wants to do with the doll and how much that composition doll means to them.

It is *strongly* advised that before anyone has a doll repaired, ask to see a sample of workmanship.

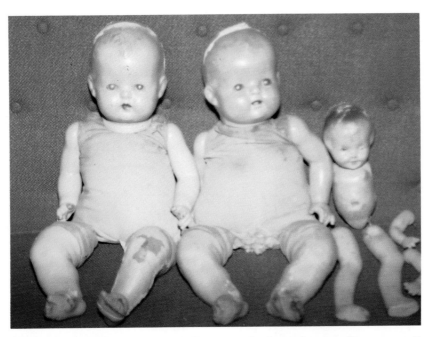

Twin composition and cloth dolls in need of repair as well as a small SALLY from the Acme Doll Co. Most people would throw these out or sell them for parts at an extremely low price because of the cost of excellent composition repair. *Courtesy Betty Barclift.*

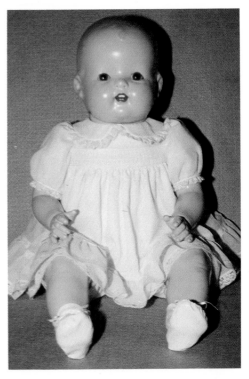

These are the dolls shown above repaired and ready to dress. The quality of workmanship is amazing and would detract very little from the original value. Repaired by owner, Betty Barclift.

This repaired composition appears to be "original." To repair, the paint must be removed down to the composition, then layered back on by dipping or airbrushing. The cleaning process is tedious and **expensive.** *Courtesy Betty Barclift.*

10½" LITTLE MISS GINGER was added to the Cosmopoliton line in 1957. These dolls are all vinyl with sleep eyes, rooted hair, jointed waist, and high heel feet. Both dolls are all original. Dolls were actually made by Doll Bodies, Inc. who also made "blanks" for other companies. Each - $95.00 up. *Courtesy Marie Ernst.*

10½" LITTLE MISS GINGER is all original in her original box. A rare find. $165.00. *Courtesy Maureen Fukushima.*

Window box packaged outfit for GINGER. It is #960, a coat and bonnet with fur trim. $12.00 up. *Courtesy Maureen Fukushima.*

These 8" dolls were sold as "blanks" to different firms to dress and market. In the center is PAM, sold through Active Doll Co. The two others are GINGER dolls marketed by the Cosmopoliton Company. They were also sold to Fortune Toys and Virga (Beehler Arts). Each - $95.00 up. *Courtesy Kris Lundquist.* (For details about Cosmopoliton, see *Modern Collector Dolls, Volume 7,* pg. 76.)

11½" Suntan Heather of 1989 has painted features, open/closed smiling mouth, blonde painted eyebrows, a hole in one ear for earring, and bendable knees. Head marked "Creata/1988" and body marked "China/Creata/1987." Original - $25.00.

11½" all vinyl doll with bendable knees and long rooted hair with blonde streak running through it. Came with bathing suit, shoes, sunglasses, and sand chair. Head marked "Creata/1988" and body marked "China/Creata/1982." $25.00.

⌐ Daddy Long Legs ⌐

There has been a great interest in the Daddy Long Legs dolls, but as with all makers, it seems the very first are the most in demand. The following list will only include up to 1992.

	Issued	Number made	Retired	Price
Boy Pig	1/90	?	12/90	$650.00
Cat in Jumpsuit	6/90	66	12/90	$725.00
Indian (first edition)	1/90	304	12/90	$800.00
Mimi	1/90	425	12/90	$900.00
Santa	1/90	48	12/90	$985.00 up
Santa (red velvet)	6/90	25	12/90	$1,500.00 up
Santa (tapestry)	6/90	25	12/90	$1,500.00 up
Wedding Rabbits	6/90	3 sets	7/90	$2,500.00 up

	Issued	Number made	Retired	Price
Goats (boy & girl)	6/90	109 & 154	12/91	$550.00
Raccoon	6/90	123	6/91	$550.00 up
Santa (black & white)	6/91	311 & 511	12/91	$385.00
Uncle Sam (white)	1/91	729	12/91	$900.00 up
Daphne	6/91		12/92	$245.00
Iris	6/91	992	12/92	$200.00
James The Groom	1/92	1,295	12/92	$285.00
Kitty Kat	1/91	527	6/92	$300.00
Lucky The Gambler	1/92	939	12/92	$325.00
Mamie the Pig	6/90	425	6/92	$425.00
Olivia	1/92	1,295	12/92	$285.00
Rachael	1/90	377	6/92	$145.00
Robby Rabbit	1/90	529	6/92	$275.00
Rose Rabbit	1/90	684	6/92	$485.00
Roxanne Rabbit	6/90	351	6/92	$350.00
Rudy Rabbit	1/90	547	6/92	$450.00
Santa	7/92	213	12/92	$365.00
Sofie	6/90	5,548	6/92	$345.00

Left: KITTY KAT made from January 1991 to June 1992. 527 made. $300.00. Right: MAMIE THE PIG was made from June 1990 to June 1992. 425 made. Also dressed in green, 1990–1992. Each - $425.00. *Courtesy Chelsey Holshoe.*

THE RABBIT FAMILY: RUDY RABBIT, the father (upper left), 547 made; ROSE RABBIT, the mother (upper right), 684 made; ROXANNE RABBIT, the sister (lower left), 351 made; and ROBBY RABBIT, the brother (lower right), 529 made. All were issued in January 1990 and retired in June 1992. RUDY - $450.00; ROSE - $485.00; ROXANNE - $350.00; ROBBY - $275.00. *Courtesy Chelsey Holshoe.*

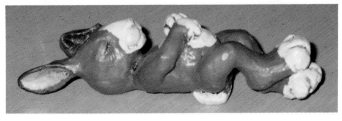

This is the baby that goes with THE RABBIT FAMILY. One piece figure is made of resin. $75.00 up. *Courtesy Chelsey Holshoe.*

Left: HUGH HOOFER was made from June 1990 to March 1994. 1,453 made. $200.00. Right: ABIGAIL THE COW was made from January 1990 to March 1995. 1,063 made in red check dress; 3,498 in blue check dress. In blue - $145.00; red - $200.00. *Courtesy Chelsey Holshoe.*

SOFIE was the first black child and was made from June 1990 to June 1992. 5,548 made. $345.00.

Courtsey Chelsey Holshoe.

DOC MOSES was made from January 1992 to September 1993. 2,494 made. $265.00. *Courtesy Chelsey Holshoe.*

SISTER MARY KATHLEEN was made from January 1991 to March 1994. 1,844 made. $265.00. *Courtesy Chelsey Holshoe.*

JACKIE is quite the lady! Made from June 1993 to December 1995. $125.00. *Courtesy Chelsey Holshoe.*

BILLYE was issued in January 1993 and retired in March 1995. 1,863 made. $195.00. *Courtesy Chelsey Holshoe.*

Green face WITCH HAZEL is 30" tall. Issued June 1990 and retired March 1995. 1,791 made. $225.00. *Courtesy Chelsey Holshoe.*

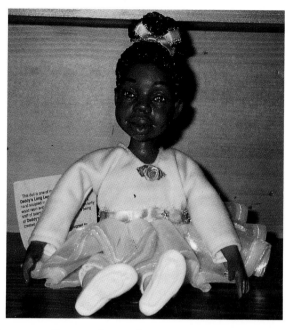

SISSY was first on the market in June 1994 and retired March 1995. 1,963 made. $195.00. *Courtesy Chelsey Holshoe.*

28" TUBBIN' SANTA comes with metal tub to put his foot in. Made from June 1994 to June 1995. $265.00 up. *Courtesy Chelsey Holshoe.*

Left: PHOEBE was put on the market in January 1993 and retired in September 1995. Right: MRS. HATTIE was first on the market in January 1991 and no retirement date has been set. Both have current value. *Courtesy Chelsey Holshoe.*

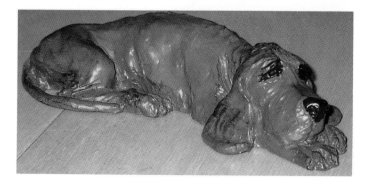

JAKE THE DOG and PUFF THE CAT look cute with any Daddy Long Legs setting. Each - $75.00 up. *Courtesy Chelsey Holshoe.*

16¾" PAVLOVA PRIMA BALLERINA from the Elegante Collection by R. Dakin. Made of all vinyl with painted features and rooted hair. It would be great to know who scultured this doll, but no information is available. Original price was $79.95. Valued now at $175.00. *Courtesy Pat Graff.*

22" SUNNY with auburn braids and LOVEY with thick black braids are from the SQUEAKEY CHEEKS doll collection by Dakin. Their bodies and limbs are made of a linen-like material. Faces and hands are made of a pink satin knit material. Both have large formed smiles and plastic upward set eyes with stitched eyelashes. Tag on bodies state "Anne Klocks design. Dakin & Co. San Francisco 1983/1984." SUNNY carries a sun; LOVEY, a large heart. Other dolls in the set were PENGUINA with a little penguin, BEARISSA with a bear, and CUP CAKE. Each retailed for $99.95. Valued now at $125.00 each.

Courtesy Jessie Smith.

⮞ Deluxe Reading ⮜

The dolls by Deluxe Reading are also marked Deluxe Topper, Topper Corp., Topper Toys, Deluxe Toy Creations, and Deluxe Premium Corp.

Some of their more collectible dolls were in the Dawn and Friends series. The entire collection may be seen mint in the box in *Modern Collector Dolls, Volume 2,* pages 62–69. It must be noted that Dawn dolls can be marked with the following numbers, but there could possibly be some others: 343/S11A, 186/A11A, 4/H57, 4/ZH129, 4/H68, 4/H78, 4/H 122, 4/H/89, 4/H 111, 4/ZH137/, 4/H57, 4/H84. Some of these numbers will have different hairdos, eye colors, or lip colors.

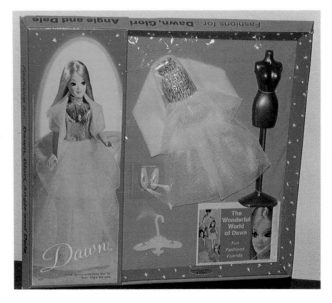

Package outfit for Dawn and friends, "Gold Glow Swirl," no. 0721, made in 1969. $15.00. *Courtesy Gloria Anderson.*

Dawn outfit, "Bell Bottom Flounce," no. 0717, was made in 1969. $10.00. *Courtesy Gloria Anderson.*

"Singing in the Rain," no. 0724, was made in 1969. $10.00. *Courtesy Gloria Anderson.*

"Blue Bell," no. 0722, was made in 1969. If not mint in box, the silver stole is generally missing. $15.00. *Courtesy Gloria Anderson.*

"Party Parfay," no. 0810, is an outfit difficult to find mint in box. $15.00. *Courtesy Gloria Anderson.*

DAWN AND FRIENDS outfit, "Down the Aisle," no. 0816, was made in 1969. $12.00. *Courtesy Gloria Anderson.*

Left: "Pink Luster," no. 8020, made in 1970. Right: "Silver Orange Slice," no. 0802, made in 1969. Each - $10.00. *Courtesy Gloria Anderson.*

"Green Fling," no. 8113, made in 1969. $12.00. *Courtesy Gloria Anderson.*

DAWN outfit "Peachy Keen," no. 0822, made in 1969. $10.00. *Courtesy Gloria Anderson.*

"What a Racket," no. 8116, made in 1970. $10.00. *Courtesy Gloria Anderson.*

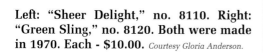

Left: "Sheer Delight," no. 8110. Right: "Green Sling," no. 8120. Both were made in 1970. Each - $10.00. *Courtesy Gloria Anderson.*

19" LUV 'N CARE made by Topper Toys. Has rooted hair and sleep eyes. Although not shown on box, doll has extra joints at the elbows. Marked on head "Deluxe Topper/1969." $35.00. *Courtesy David Spurgeon.*

Boxed outfits for PENNY BRITE. The formal has been found on many 8" BETSY McCALL dolls, and it appeared to original to them. But as far as we know, it was only made for the PENNY BRITE doll. Boxed coat set - $15.00. Boxed formal gown - $22.00. *Courtesy Sandy Johnson Barts.*

⚞ Walt Disney ⚟

It must be noted that not all the items shown in this section are authorized Disney dolls. Although these characters were popular in children's books, Walt Disney brought them to life in his full-length cartoon movies and made their personalities legends. Because of this, it is easier for collectors to locate Disney items.

Four 12" Knickerbocker Dwarf dolls – HAPPY, DOC, DOPEY, and BASHFUL. Shown with 13½" Babyland rag lady with painted face and 13" Maude Toussey Fangle baby with original dress, bonnet, and oilcloth body. Dwarfs - $200.00 each. Rag lady - $165.00. Baby - $595.00. *Courtesy Turn of Century Antiques.*

12" all stuffed cloth BASHFUL with molded oilcloth face mask. Has replaced look-alike jacket. Made by Ideal. $225.00. *Courtesy Ellen Dodge.*

15" SNOW WHITE by Mollye Goldman of Mollye Internationals. Has black human hair wig and brown eyes painted to side. Cloth body and limbs with mask face. Underskirt has lightened from a deeper purple. Label sewn to leg states "Mollye-'es" in script, along with "product. American made." $195.00 up. *Courtesy Pat Graff.*

14" all vinyl SNOW WHITE was made in 1988 by Robin Woods. Has apple attached to skirt. $125.00. *Courtesy Pat Graff.*

8" SNOW WHITE was made in 1983 by Ideal. Doll is original and in mint condition. $35.00. *Courtesy Pat Graff.*

18" SNOW WHITE with cloth body, vinyl wigged head, and vinyl limbs. Has beaded slippers and attached apple. Made by Gotz in 1989. $175.00. *Courtesy Pat Graff.*

8" SNOW WHITE with blue painted eyes and black wig. Designed by Robin Woods and made for Disney World and Disneyland in 1990. $165.00. *Courtesy Pat Graff.*

19" vinyl SNOW WHITE was designed and made by Susan Wakeen in 1992. A limited edition of 2,500. $250.00. *Courtesy Pat Graff.*

15" porcelain SNOW WHITE with cloth body and painted eyes. This original doll was made by Maryanne Oldenburg in 1992 and was a limited edition of 30. $585.00. *Courtesy Pat Graff.*

13" porcelain SNOW WHITE was designed and made by Wendy Lawton in 1993. Taken from story when Snow White cleaned the dwarfs' home. A limited edition of 500. $500.00. *Courtesy Pat Graff.*

19" SNOW WHITE was designed by Shirley Peck for America Beauty in 1994. She is made of felt with oil-painted features. A limited edition of 100. Original - $325.00. *Courtesy Pat Graff.*

11½" SNOW WHITE made by Effanbee in 1993. Has inset eyes and rooted hair. All original. $55.00. *Courtesy Pat Graff.*

14" vinyl CINDERELLA AT THE BALL has special slipper and pillow. Made by Robin Woods in 1990. $165.00. *Courtesy Pat Graff.*

These LOLLIPOP TWINS look at each other as if the other had the best lollipop! Made of resin by CHAYE AROTSKY. Marked "Sara." Each - $38.00.

13" HENRY by ANRI is made of maple wood with extra joints at knees and elbows. Has wig and painted eyes. Shoes are part of doll. Limited edition of 1,000. $650.00. *Courtesy Pat Graff.*

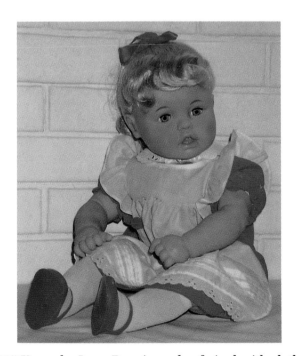

21" KAREN by LASSI BATZ is made of vinyl with cloth body. Has rooted hair and sleep eyes with lashes. Ordered from Spiegel's catalog in 1989. $95.00. *Courtesy Pat Graff.*

28" reproduction of artist doll with cloth body and porcelain limbs and head. Has set glass eyes, inset long eyelashes, and closed mouth. Original sculptor's name not known. The only mark is "ART MOLD COMPANY." (A lady near Dallas, TX, put the doll together, painted and dressed it, then sold it to a dealer.) Current value - $150.00 (cost $500.00).

20" CANDY is made of porcelain with a cloth body. Has rooted hair and inset eyes with lashes. Made by YOLANDO BELLO in 1990. $775.00. *Courtesy Pat Graff.*

22" NINET made of vinyl and cloth with inset eyes, rooted hair, and good character face. Made by BERJUSA of Spain in 1990. Original - $800.00. *Courtesy Pat Graff.*

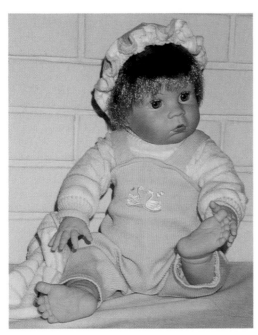

18" all vinyl AMY with extra joints at waist and upper arms and thighs. Has inset eyes with lashes. Made by BERJUSA of Spain. Original was the 1989 "Doll Concept of the Year" award winner from *Doll Reader* magazine. Face is international copy of GUM DROP made by Boots Tyner. $80.00. *Courtesy Pat Graff.*

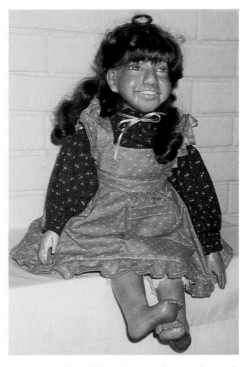

23" LUCY is made of handcarved maple with cloth body and painted features. Made in limited production by NANCY BRUNS (BRUNSWOOD DOLLS) in 1986. LUCY has a brother, TIM, and both are portraits of sculptor's children. Original - $385.00. *Courtesy Pat Graff.*

10" jointed wooden doll with painted features made by HELEN BULLARD. Original dress labeled "Helen Bullard's Handmade Original." Sold through Kimport Dolls for $12.50. $150.00. *Courtesy Susan Girardot.*

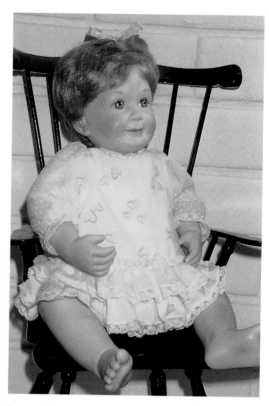

12" (seated) AMY made by SONJA BRYER in 1994. Made of porcelain with cloth body and painted eyes. Not sold with a box. This is the prototype of a limited edition of 10. Original - $385.00. *Courtesy Pat Graff.*

20½" GEORGE and 19" MARTHA WASHINGTON designed, made, and dressed by EMMA CLEAR in the late 1940s. Pair - $895.00. *Courtesy Turn of Century Antiques.*

15" painted latex doll sculptured and made by DEEWEES COCHRON in the 1930s. It is a "look-alike" doll that has been much loved by the child-owner. She is a doll of beauty *because* of the love shown her. $850.00 up. *Courtesy Susan Girardot.*

21" MAYA is made of vinyl with cloth body. Sleep eyes have lashes. Made by COROLLE in 1988 with a limited edition of 500 signed. **$285.00.** *Courtesy Pat Graff.*

21" HELENE is made of vinyl with cloth body. Sleep eyes have lashes. Made by COROLLE in 1987 with a limited edition of 750 signed. **$300.00.** *Courtesy Pat Graff.*

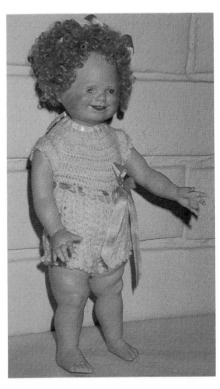

18" LADY GABRIELLE is made of porcelain with a cloth body. She is from the EUGENIA DUKAS Collection of 1988. **$350.00.** *Courtesy Pat Graff.*

9" JUDY was made by SUSAN DUNHAM in 1993 and has a limited edition of 50. Made of porcelain and is jointed at the neck and shoulders only. Has intaglio eyes. Original - **$225.00.** *Courtesy Pat Graff.*

12" doll made by ENGEL-PUPPEN in the 1980s, name unknown. Made of vinyl with cloth body. Sleep eyes have lashes. Hair made to be this way. $95.00. *Courtesy Pat Graff.*

18" DOROTHEA made by ENGEL-PUPPEN in 1989. Made of cloth and vinyl. Has sleep eyes with lashes. $135.00. *Courtesy Pat Graff.*

19" LOUISE made by ENGEL-PUPPEN of Germany in 1988. Made of vinyl with cloth body. Has sleep eyes with lashes. $145.00. *Courtesy Pat Graff.*

19" ALEX made of vinyl and cloth. Has sleep eyes with lashes. Made by ENGEL-PUPPEN of Germany in 1988. $135.00. *Courtesy Pat Graff.*

24" ROSEL by CHRISTEL FLORCHINGER of Germany in 1991. Made of vinyl and cloth with human hair and inset eyes with lashes. $685.00. *Courtesy Pat Graff.*

19" SOIREE is part of the Biribiki Series made by FURGA in 1992. Made of vinyl with rooted hair. Eyes and lashes are painted. $150.00. *Courtesy Pat Graff.*

28" MARLENE designed by Rotraut Schrott for GADCO (Great American Doll Co.) in 1990. Made of vinyl with cloth body. Has inset eyes with lashes. Came with dog, tagged "Popcorn, The Great American Dog." Production stopped in 1992. $500.00. *Courtesy Pat Graff.*

18½" MILLICENT is one of the KALICO KIDS made by SUZANNE GIBSON in 1973. Made of vinyl with cloth body and painted eyes. Signed on body. Original and in mint condition. $50.00 up. *Courtesy Pat Graff.*

8" MEXICO made by SUZANNE GIBSON in 1984. Limited edition of 1,000 signed. The 1984 set price was $90.00. Valued now at $125.00. *Courtesy Roger Jones.*

9" RAIN, RAIN, GO AWAY made by SUZANNE GIBSON in 1988. Made of vinyl with sleep eyes, lashes, and rooted hair. $55.00. *Courtesy Pat Graff.*

16½" LITTLE MISS MUFFET made by SUZANNE GIBSON in 1985. Made of vinyl with cloth body. $95.00. *Courtesy Pat Graff.*

12" all vinyl GRACE ANNE GOODHUE COOLIDGE is part of the President's Ladies series designed by SUZANNE GIBSON. Made in 1985. $100.00 up. *Courtesy Pat Graff.*

12" all vinyl PRESIDENT LADIES designed by SUZANNE GIBSON. Left: LOUISA CATHERINE JOHNSON ADAMS from 1987. Center: MAMIE DOUD EISENHOWER from 1986. Right: ANGELICA SINGLETON VAN BUREN from 1986. Each - $100.00 up.

Courtesy Pat Graff.

22" vinyl CHRISTMAS COOKIE with inset eyes and lashes. She was made as GOOD-KRUGER'S 1990 Christmas doll and has a limited edition of 1,000 signed. $265.00.

Courtesy Pat Graff.

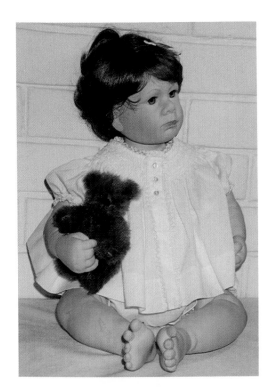

20" HUG BUG was made as a special limited edition of 1,000 by GOOD-KRUGER in 1989. Made of vinyl with cloth body. Has inset eyes with lashes. Came with teddy bear. $285.00. *Courtesy Pat Graff.*

Left: 21" LOVE ME FOR CHRISTMAS was the GOOD-KRUGER doll for Christmas 1989. Made of vinyl with inset eyes and lashes. Limited to 2,000 signed. $265.00. *Courtesy Pat Graff.*

Below: 17" RAMBLIN' ROSIE made by GOOD-KRUGER in 1993. Made of vinyl with inset eyes and lashes. Limited to 1,500 signed. Doll did not market well. The same doll was made in porcelain but with different name. $295.00. *Courtesy Pat Graff.*

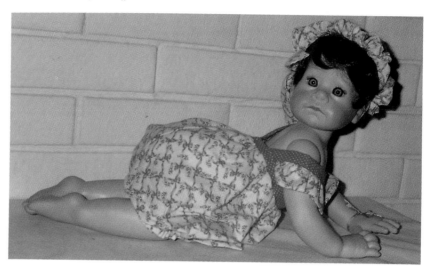

18" LEE was made by GOTZ in 1987. Made of vinyl with cloth body. $125.00. *Courtesy Pat Graff.*

16" ANTJE was made in 1988 for the MARIANNE GOTZ Design Collection and limited to 300. Made of vinyl and cloth with painted eyes and hair lashes. $285.00. *Courtesy Pat Graff.*

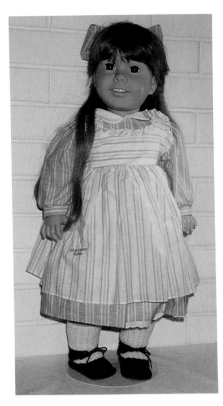

24" SILKE was made for the MARIANNE GOTZ Design Collection in 1988. Made of vinyl with cloth body. Has sleep eyes with lashes. Limited to 300. $365.00.

Courtesy Pat Graff.

This 20" doll was designed by SYLVIA NATTERER for GOTZ in 1988, and it was the first in the Fanouche Series. $300.00. *Courtesy Pat Graff.*

25" MARCEL was made in 1990 by GOTZ. Made of vinyl with cloth body and painted eyes. The sculpture was by Sylvia Natterer. $465.00. *Courtesy Pat Graff.*

16½" AMILY made of vinyl with cloth body. Has sleep eyes with lashes. Made by GOTZ in 1991. $135.00. *Courtesy Pat Graff.*

15" JONATHON was designed by Sylvia Natterer for GOTZ in 1991. Made of vinyl with painted eyes. $175.00. *Courtesy Pat Graff.*

24" ALESSANDRA was designed by Philip Heath for GOTZ and was the D.O.T.Y. (Doll of the Year) winner in 1992. Made of vinyl with molded torso and cloth body. $600.00. *Courtesy Pat Graff.*

20" vinyl ELENA was designed by Sylvia Natterer in 1992 and made by GOTZ. $300.00. *Courtesy Pat Graff.*

24" AMI was designed by Philip Heath for GOTZ in 1992. Made of rigid vinyl with a cloth midsection. She has inset eyes. $600.00. *Courtesy Pat Graff.*

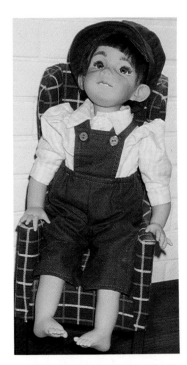

20" and 9" TERESA AND BABY JUANITA designed by Sylvia Natterer for GOTZ in 1992. Limited to 1,500 signed. Set - $625.00. *Courtesy Pat Graff.*

21" vinyl XAVIER with cloth body, set eyes, and full lashes. Has very protuding ears. Limited to 1,000. Made in 1990 by GROSSLE-SCHMIDT. $525.00. *Courtesy Pat Graff.*

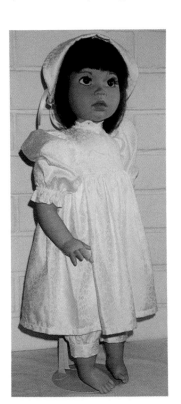

21" LIN made by GROSSLE-SCHMIDT in 1990. Made of vinyl with cloth body. Has inset eyes with lashes. Limited to 1,000. $525.00. *Courtesy Pat Graff.*

24" porcelain BUMBL with cloth body. Made by GROSSLE-SCHMIDT in 1993 and limited to 300. $1,785.00. *Courtesy Pat Graff.*

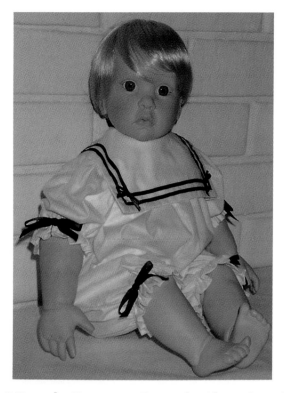

13" TRACY made by JAN HAGARA in 1986. Made of porcelain with cloth body and inset eyes. $250.00.
Courtesy Pat Graff.

16" KAREN by HILDEGARDE GUNZEL for Alexander Doll Company in 1990. Made of vinyl with cloth body and inset eyes. $165.00. *Courtesy Pat Graff.*

12" PABLO and 16" BLANCA designed by HILDEGARDE GUNZEL in 1991 and 1993 for the Alexander Doll Company. 12" - $100.00; 16" - $200.00. *Courtesy Pat Graff.*

16" ERICA and 12" KATIE designed by HILDEGARDE GUNZEL in 1990 and 1992 for the Alexander Doll Company. 16" - $175.00; 12" - $125.00. *Courtesy Pat Graff.*

Two HILDEGARDE GUNZEL designs for the Alexander Doll Company – 12" LOTUS from 1993 and 16" YAM from 1991. Both are made of vinyl. 12" - $125.00; 16" - $200.00. *Courtesy Pat Graff.*

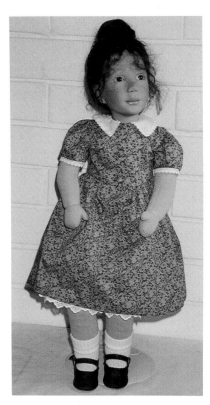

20" LISBETH made by SONJA HARTMAN in 1993. Has vinyl head with cloth body and limbs. $365.00. *Courtesy Pat Graff.*

21" ALLISON made by CHRISTINE HEATH-ORANGE of England in 1992. Made of porcelain with cloth body. Inset eyes have lashes. Limited to 25. This is the first doll made by Philip Heath's ex-wife. $1,450.00. *Courtesy Pat Graff.*

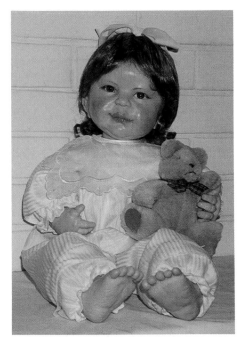

24" unnamed baby made by ROLANDA HEIMER of Germany in 1990. Made of cernit with cloth body. Has glass eyes with lashes. Wig was originally black mohair, but former owner changed to this one. Real baby outfit tagged "West Germany." One of a kind with certificate. $2,800.00. *Courtesy Pat Graff.*

7½" TWO TOUGH HOMBRES was designed and made by CANDY HUND of Candy's Characters in 1993. Has fimo head, hands, and boots. Eyes are inset. Doll included horse and bear. One of a kind doll creation. $525.00. *Courtesy Pat Graff.*

24" BRIANNA made by ELKE HUTCHINS in 1991. Made of porcelain with cloth body. Inset eyes have lashes. Limited to 400. $800.00. *Courtesy Pat Graff.*

24" BRAELYN made by ELKE HUTCHINS in 1991. Won both the Doll of the Year Award and *Dolls* Magazine Award in 1991. Limited to 400. $1,500.00. *Courtesy Pat Graff.*

16" BRENT made by MAGGIE IACANO in 1993. Made of felt and jointed at neck, elbows, knees, and ankles, plus usual joints. Has painted features. Limited to 75. $685.00. *Courtesy Pat Graff.*

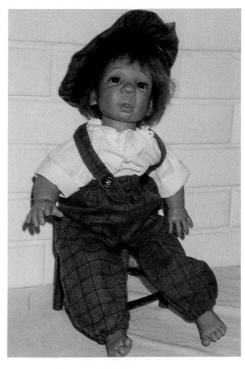

17" MATTHEW by JECKLE-JENSON in 1992. Made of vinyl with cloth body. Has inset eyes with lashes and mohair wig. Later dolls that look like this were put out by The Doll Factory and named Rotten Kids. $385.00. *Courtesy Pat Graff.*

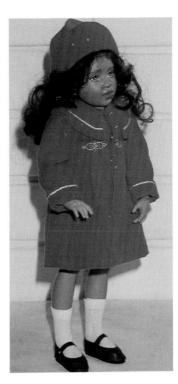

Dolls from the "When We Were Little Girls" series by HELEN KISH. Left: 10½" KELSEY made in 1991, represents the 1970s. $325.00. Center: 10" MARY KATE made in 1991, represents the 1950s. $325.00. Right: 10½" SUGAR made in 1993, represents the 1920s. $255.00. (Also see group picture in *Modern Collectors Dolls, Volume 7*, pg. 103.)
Courtesy Pat Graff.

10" ANDIE made by HELEN KISH in the 1990s. Has painted eyes and open/closed laughing mouth. $325.00. *Courtesy Pat Graff.*

20" unnamed boy and girl by PAT KOLESAR in 1980. Both are made of cloth with human hair wigs and inset eyes and lashes. Tag is sewn on. Each have a limited edition of 10. Each - $185.00. *Courtesy Pat Graff.*

22" JULIET IRIS made by BARBARA LARSON in 1990. She is made of porcelain with a cloth body. Inset eyes have lashes. $585.00. *Courtesy Pat Graff.*

22" CHELSEA ROSE made by BARBARA LARSON in 1990. She is made of porcelain with a cloth body. Inset eyes have lashes. Limited to 50. $485.00. *Courtesy Pat Graff.*

13" NANTHY by WENDY LAWTON in 1988. Made of all porcelain with glass eyes and human hair wig. Limited edition of 500. Original and in mint condition. $425.00. *Courtesy Pat Graff.*

12" BONNIE (FIRST BIRTHDAY) by WENDY LAWTON in 1990. Made of porcelain and has inset eyes. Limited to 500. $325.00. *Courtesy Pat Graff.*

WENDY LAWTON's designs for the Ashton-Drake Galleries' *Little Women* Series from 1995. Dolls are made of porcelain and cloth. Top left: BETH; top right: AMY (with original hair net over face); bottom left: MEG; bottom right: JO. AMY kneels (sits) so the collector is able to make a nice grouping out of the dolls. Each - $70.00. *Courtesy Roger Jones.*

21" ANNE-SOPHIE made by HELOISE (JOELLE LEMASSON) of France in 1990. Made of resin with cloth body and has enameled painted eyes. $425.00. *Courtesy Pat Graff.*

6½" HITTY from R. Fields' collection, "Hitty, Her First Hundred Years." This excellent example was carved by MARY LU LUNDSTROM in 1993. Doll is jointed and has painted hair and features. $85.00. *Courtesy Roger Jones.*

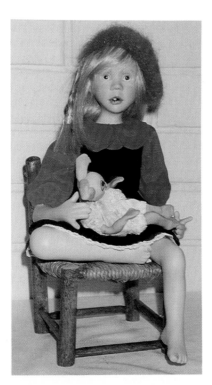

11" porcelain NICOLE by SANDY MCASLYN is posed in a seated position and came with chair and bunny. Has cloth body and painted eyes. Limited to 100. $450.00.

Courtesy Pat Graff.

Seated 8" DYLAN made by SANDY MCASLYN in 1992. Made of porcelain with painted eyes. Limited to 100. $465.00. *Courtesy Pat Graff.*

8" CARLIE made by JERRI MCCLOUD (DOLLS BY JERRI) in 1991. Made of vinyl with inset eyes. $95.00. *Courtesy Pat Graff.*

8" GIGI made by JERRI MCCLOUD (DOLLS BY JERRI) in 1991. Made of porcelain with inset eyes. $300.00. *Courtesy Pat Graff.*

17" MARIAH made by JERRI MCCLOUD (DOLLS BY JERRI) in 1991. Made of porcelain with inset eyes and lashes. Limited to 450. $385.00. *Courtesy Pat Graff.*

15" CLARA AND THE NUTCRACKER made by CINDY MCCLURE (VICTORIA IMPEX) in 1989. Made of porcelain with cloth body and inset eyes. Limited edition of 600. Original - $245.00. *Courtesy Pat Graff.*

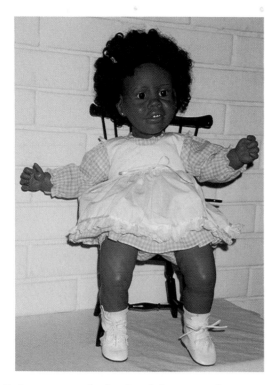

21" AMANDA made by LEE MIDDLETON in 1987 and retired in 1989. She is made of vinyl with a cloth body. $275.00. *Courtesy Pat Graff.*

24" MOUNTAIN CHILD commemorates the May 18, 1980, eruption of Mount St. Helen. Has "Mt. Babies" incised on porcelain head. Wears knitted sweater, cap, and socks, linen shorts, and hiking boots. Her backpack contains a pre-eruption map of the mountain, a vial of ash, a photo of the eruption, and a lined, quilted sleeping bag made to scale. Doll was made by MOUNTAIN BABIES DOLL FACTORY in Graham, Washington. Limited to 100 dolls. $700.00.

24" ARIEL made by JANET NESS in 1990. Made of porcelain with cloth body and inset eyes with lashes. This is the second doll made by this artist. Limited to 250. $800.00 up. *Courtesy Pat Graff.*

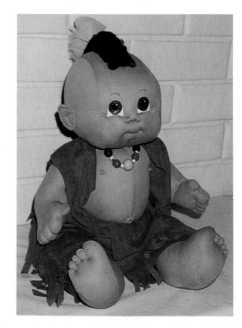

16" OKIE DOKIE is a cloth soft sculptured doll with painted eyes and rooted hair. Purchased at Choctaw Reservation store in Oklahoma City in 1991. Has birth certificate but no box. Doll signed by LORI OLSEN. $85.00. *Courtesy Pat Graff.*

18" ORIENTAL GIRL, #86-88-145, made by HEIDI OTT in 1988. Rigid vinyl construction with human hair wig. $700.00. *Courtesy Pat Graff.*

22" BRENT made by PHYLLIS PARKINS in 1992. Made of vinyl with cloth body. Inset eyes have lashes. Limited to 2,500. $250.00. *Courtesy Pat Graff.*

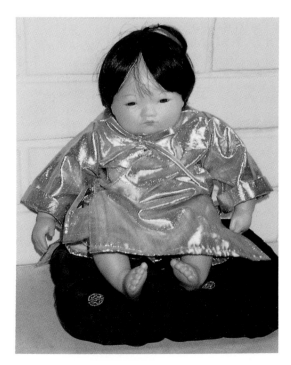

14" porcelain LITTLE EMPEROR with cloth body and inset eyes. Came with cushion. Made by DOLLS BY PAULINE in 1990. Limited edition (number unknown). $260.00. *Courtesy Pat Graff.*

15" ALICIA made of vinyl with cloth body. Inset eyes have lashes. Can suck thumb. Made by DOLL BY PAULINE in 1991. $90.00. *Courtesy Pat Graff.*

14" NATASYA (RUSSIA) made by DOLLS BY PAULINE in 1991. Made of porcelain with cloth body and inset eyes. Limited to 1,500. $275.00. *Courtesy Pat Graff.*

14" LIBERTY (AMERICA) made by DOLLS BY PAULINE in 1991. Made of porcelain with cloth body and inset eyes. Limited to 1,500. $265.00. *Courtesy Pat Graff.*

14" porcelain LING LING (CHINA) with cloth body and inset eyes. Made by DOLLS BY PAULINE in 1992. Limited to 1,500. $265.00. *Courtesy Pat Graff.*

18" AMELIA has one-piece porcelain head and shoulderplate, cloth body, and inset eyes. Made by DOLLS BY PAULINE in 1992. Limited to 2,500. $265.00. *Courtesy Pat Graff.*

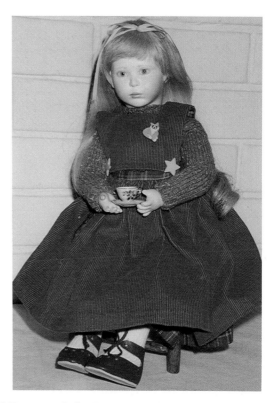

17" PATTI-ANN made by HAL PAYNE in 1993. Has stoneware head, hands, and feet. Wooden body has extra joints at knees and elbows. Eyes are inset. Limited to 50. $1,700.00. *Courtesy Pat Graff.*

15" BETH made by LYNN AND MICHAEL ROCHE in 1992. Has wooden ball joints at elbows and knees, jointed wrists, and inset eyes. Cup and saucer added. $675.00. *Courtesy Pat Graff.*

17" vinyl SOPHIE with cloth body, painted eyes, and wire armature for posing. Made by ROTHKIRCH in 1992. $265.00. *Courtesy Pat Graff.*

10½" MARGARET O'BRIEN made by ROTHSCHILD in 1987. Made of hard plastic with jointed knees and elbows. Painted features and mohair wig. $55.00. *Courtesy Pat Graff.*

5" to 16" GERMAN FAMILY that is so much like the LaFamille Bella that one wonders which came first. (La Bella can be seen in *Modern Collector Dolls, Volume 5*, pg. 128.) Father is named Thomas; mother, Tina; daughter, Susi; and baby, Tommy. Box is marked "Schildkrot." Parents have extra joints at elbows and knees. Dolls and clothes are of excellent quality. Set - $285.00. *Courtesy Betty Shriver.*

17" INGA made by KAREN SCHMELING. This one-of-a-kind doll is made of cernit and cloth with inset eyes. **$700.00.** *Courtesy Pat Graff.*

24" ANNA made by VERA SCHOLZ (WALTERHAUSEN PUPPENMANUFAKUR, GMBH Germany) in 1993. Made of rigid vinyl with cloth body. Inset eyes have lashes. Excellent quality doll and clothes. Limited to 3,000. **$725.00.** *Courtesy Pat Graff.*

14" SALA and **BERG** made by SEKIGUCHI (Japan) and distributed by Mattel. They are made of vinyl and cloth and have eyes with no pupils. (May be seen in different oufits in *Modern Collectors Dolls, Volume 7,* page 220.) Limited to 2,000. Each - $95.00. *Courtesy Pat Graff.*

18" LA CHERE made by SEKIGUCHI in 1983. Made of vinyl and cloth with inset eyes. Limited to 1,800. **$95.00.** *Courtesy Pat Graff.*

20" porcelain JOHANNA with cloth body and sleep eyes. Made by SIGIKID in 1989. Limited to 100. $250.00. *Courtesy Pat Graff.*

19" KATHI made by SIGIKID in 1990. Made of vinyl and cloth with painted eyes. $295.00. *Courtesy Pat Graff.*

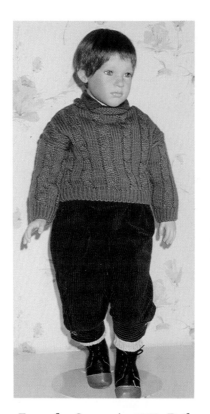

24" ALMUTH and SAMMY designed by SABINE ESCHE for SIGIKID in 1990. Both are made of vinyl and cloth with painted eyes. Girl was the Doll of the Year winner for 1990. Boy has same face as girl, but suits the boy better. Almuth - $650.00. Sammy - $725.00. *Courtesy Pat Graff.*

20" ANNETTE made by SIGIKID in 1990. Made of vinyl and cloth with painted eyes. Designed as a play doll. $325.00. *Courtesy Pat Graff.*

24" WINONA I designed by SABINE ESCHE for SIGIKID in 1991. Made of vinyl with cloth body. Limited to 750. $750.00. *Courtesy Pat Graff.*

22" GABI II designed by GABRIELE BRAUN for SIGIKID in 1992. Made of vinyl with cloth body and painted eyes. Limited to 750. $800.00. *Courtesy Pat Graff.*

11" TIM and NADJA designed by WILTRUD STEIN for SIGIKID in 1992. Made of vinyl and cloth with painted eyes. Limited to 500. Each - $350.00. *Courtesy Pat Graff.*

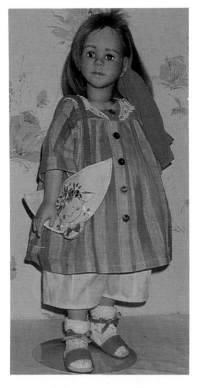

21" NIKKI designed by ANGELIKA MANNERSDORFER for SIGIKID in 1993. Made of vinyl with cloth body and painted eyes. Limited to 500. $650.00 up. *Courtesy Pat Graff.*

13" TIMID BALLERINA is a handcarved wooden doll by PAUL SPENCER. She has carved hair, painted eyes, and extra joints at elbows and knees. Limited to 25 or less. $1,200.00 up.

13½" ALICIA made by JOYCE STAFFORD. She is made of porcelain with cloth body. Marked "Alicia/Joyce Stafford/NIADA/1980." $550.00. *Courtesy Pat Graff.*

17" MARGIT made by STEIFF of Germany in 1987. She is made of all cloth with painted features. $525.00.

Courtesy Pat Graff.

19" CHARLOTTE made by MADELEINE NEILL-ST. CLAIR in 1992. Made of porcelain with cloth body and inset eyes. Limited to 25. $1,100.00. *Courtesy Pat Graff.*

14" JUNITA made by STUPSI of Germany in 1984. Made of all cloth with plastic button eyes. All original. $125.00. *Courtesy Pat Graff.*

33" AMBER LAUREN made by CHARLEEN THANOS in 1994. Made of porcelain and cloth. Was available with this doll, also designed by Thanos, or with kitten. $2,800.00 up. *Courtesy Charleen Thanos.*

28" PAIGE – the child any grandmother would spoil! Made of porcelain and cloth with glass eyes. Made by Charleen Thanos in 1994. Each - $1,500.00. *Courtesy Charleen Thanos.*

31" ZOEY BRIDE who made a grand entrance into the Toy Fair in 1995. She has also been seen in one of the most exclusive store windows in the country. Designed and made by CHARLEEN THANOS. $3,200.00 up. *Courtesy Charleen Thanos.*

29" STEFFI made by CHARLEEN THANOS in 1995. She is the birthday girl and carries a cake that opens with a birthday message. Price unknown. *Courtesy Charleen Thanos.*

31" ZOEY VICTORIA is the cousin of ZOEY BRIDE and beautiful in her own right. There is no envy between these two young ladies. Original by CHARLEEN THANOS. **$3,600.00 up.** *Courtesy Charleen Thanos.*

33" SWAN was made by CHARLEEN THANOS in 1995. This wonderful porcelain and cloth child doll can be of many races. Here she is a lovely Oriental girl. With her hat on, she looks like a turn of the century child from Cuba or Argentina. (For comparison, see hatted version in *Patricia Smith's Doll Values, Twelfth Edition,* pg. 217.) **Price unknown.** *Courtesy Charleen Thanos.*

16" Corey made by **Louise Tierney** in 1990. Made of vinyl and cloth with inset eyes. Has twin sister, **Tonya**, with same face. **$185.00.** *Courtesy Pat Graff.*

20" American Model dolls by **Robert Tonner**. Both are made of vinyl with painted eyes. Each have a limited edition of 500. Left is **Gold Lame** from 1994, and right is **Paige** from 1995. Each - **$300.00.** *Courtesy Pat Graff.*

26½" Camilla made by **Ruth Treiffison** in 1991. Made of vinyl and cloth. Inset eyes have lashes. Limited to 1,000. **$765.00.** *Courtesy Pat Graff.*

21" Girl in Violet Dress & Red Shoes made by **Carol Trobe** in 1992. This one-of-a-kind doll was sculpted in cernit and has a hole drilled in bottom of foot for custom stand. She has inset eyes and appears to have an "attitude." **$3,250.00 up.** *Courtesy Pat Graff.*

18½" INDIAN MAN AND WOMAN by P. WACANDA. They are made of porcelain with cloth bodies and painted eyes. They are dressed as Pueblo Indians and were purchased in a Colorado shop (non-doll shop) in 1994. May have been made by someone from commerical molds. It is known that "P" in mold marks stands for Pat Wacanda, but it is not known if she sold these molds. This fact is brought up because they were purchased very reasonably in 1994 as compared to what they sold for originally on the retail market in 1989. Pair - $500.00. *Courtesy Pat Graff.*

All of these dolls were made by SUSAN WAKEEN. Left: 17½" APRIL is made of vinyl with inset eyes. Made in 1988. $150.00. Center: 20" AMBERLEE is made of vinyl and cloth. Inset eyes have lashes. Made in 1990. $185.00. Right: 16" KEVIN is from the Buttons and Beaus Series in 1989. Made of vinyl with inset eyes. Limited edition of 2,500. $175.00. *Courtesy Pat Graff.*

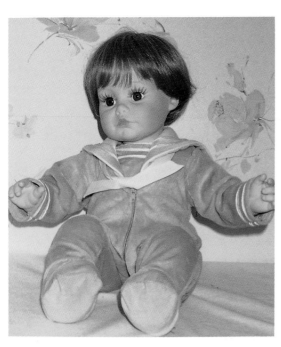

20" JASON made by SUSAN WAKEEN in 1993. Made of vinyl and cloth. Inset eyes have lashes. Limited to 2,500. $185.00. *Courtesy Pat Graff.*

9" KIMBERLY made by PHYLLIS WRIGHT in 1991. Made of porcelain and limited to 500. $300.00. *Courtesy Pat Graff.*

20" LITTLE RED RIDING HOOD made by R. JOHN WRIGHT in 1987. Made of felt with painted features and mohair wig. Limited to 500. $3,200.00 up. *Courtesy Pat Graff.*

11" MARY is a one-of-a-kind doll made by VON WALTERS in 1990. Made of mixed media, according to tag. Has painted eyes and nonremovable clothes. Made in Ohio and may have only been sold at doll shows. $175.00. *Courtesy Pat Graff.*

23" MARIE made by ZAPH in 1990. Made of vinyl and cloth. Limited to 150. $285.00. *Courtesy Pat Graff.*

18" unnamed dolls made in 1987. Made of vinyl and cloth with painted eyes. They are marked "Creation Marie-Luic" but it was understood that they were made by ZAPH, although other ZAPH dolls are marked with a "Z." Each - $95.00. *Courtesy Pat Graff.*

19" CHERI made by ZAPH in 1990. Made of vinyl and cloth. Sleep eyes have lashes. $75.00. *Courtesy Pat Graff.*

17" TIFFANY made by ZANINI-ZAMBELLI of Italy in 1989. Made of vinyl and cloth. Limited to 2,000. $125.00. *Courtesy Pat Graff.*

20" MADDIE was designed by PAT SECRIST for JOHANNES ZOOK in 1989. Made of vinyl and cloth and does not have molded tongue. Inset eyes have lashes. $185.00. *Courtesy Pat Graff.*

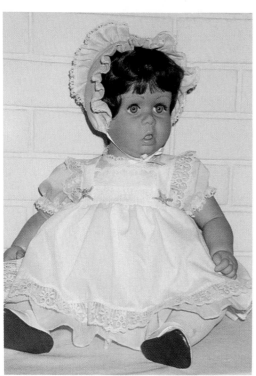

19" BRITTANY made by JOHANNES ZOOK in 1989. Made of vinyl with cloth body, inset eyes, and molded tongue. $185.00. *Courtesy Pat Graff.*

16" CHRISTMAS LOVE made by ZOOK as the 1989 Christmas dolls. Made of vinyl with glass eyes and lashes. Limited edition of 250. Pair - $475.00. *Courtesy Pat Graff.*

⪜ EEGEE ⪜

The majority of collectors hunt for or purchase celebrity dolls, and I felt a reminder should be given that EEGEE, considered a minor doll company, made a doll of Gigi Perreau — one of the most elusive dolls ever. Their hard plastic doll with a vinyl head was made in 1951. This doll ranks right along with Terri Lee's Gene Autry, Uneeda's Rita Hayworth, and Molly Goldman's Jeanette MacDonald.

Anyone who owns or is looking for this doll may like a little background information about the girl many felt would be the second

Shirley Temple. Gigi was born with a name as long as she was: Ghislaine Elizabeth Marie Theresa Perreau-Saussine. She was born in 1941 of French parents. During World War II, her parents resided in Los Angeles after fleeing the invasion of Paris. During the 1940s and 1950s, Gigi was a child star, but like Shirley Temple before her, she could not maintain her box office popularity after becoming a teen.

A photograph of the doll appears in *Modern Collector's Dolls, Volume 1* on pg 74. It also appears in the September 1952 issue of *Playthings* magazine.

These 14" GEMMETTE dolls were made by Eegee (Goldberger Mfg. Co.) in 1963. They are made of high quality vinyl with thin adult bodies and extremely pretty hands. Both are all original and have their own stands. Each - $50.00.

Courtesy Pat Graff.

7–8" HAWAIIAN BABY BUDS from the Novelty Art line made by Effanbee in 1919 to 1920. Dolls were made of composition with painted features. Inclued in the line were Eskimos, Indians, and Orientals. $165.00 up. *Courtesy Joan Guelzov.*

17" bisque PATSY, mold #127, with fired-in cafe au lait complexion, sleep eyes, and "rosebud" style mouth with teeth. She has the typical PATSY body with right arm bent at the elbow. $2,800.00. *Courtesy Turn of Century Antiques.*

20" MARY JANE made by Effanbee in 1917. She is a bisque headed doll with an open mouth and sleep eyes. Molds were made from the bisque head, and these dolls, like 14" one shown, were made until 1923. Bisque headed dolls came in 16", 18", 20", and 24" sizes and are marked. Both dolls are original. 20" - $950.00 up. 14" - $350.00 up. *Courtesy Joan Guelzov.*

18" MARY JANE from 1920 with composition head taken from bisque mold. Has fully jointed German body, sleep eyes, open mouth, and original factory clothes. $800.00 up. *Courtesy Jeanne Venner.*

24" BUBBLES by Effanbee is made of composition with a tightly stuffed body, open mouth with dimples, and sleep eyes. She is original with tagged clothes and in near mint condition. $500.00. *Courtesy Turn of Century Antiques.*

Very rare 22" PATSY LOU is a very special and happy girl. She has an open mouth with six teeth and is marked on body but not on head. Wearing original clothes and came in her original box. With box - $600.00. Doll only (mint) - $550.00. *Courtesy Martha Sweeney.*

A cute 14" composition PATSY from 1927 with molded painted hair and painted features. Has bent right elbow typical to Patsy dolls. All original. $400.00 up.

Courtesy Joan Guelzov.

16" PATSY JR. is dressed in an adorable outfit and has a wig over her molded hair. All original from 1930. $400.00 up. *Courtesy Joan Guelzov.*

9" PATSY BABYETTE is a pre-World War II doll with all cloth body and limbs. Has straight toddler style legs and celluloid gauntlet style hands. (All composition baby can be seen in *Modern Collector Dolls, Volume 6,* page 83.) **$275.00.** *Courtesy Ellen Dodge.*

9" all composition PATSYETTE with painted eyes and hair. Has original clothes except for socks and shoe strings. **$350.00 up.** *Courtesy Pat Graff.*

It is rare to find an 11" PATSYKIN/PATSY JR. with its original human hair wig, like this sandy blonde one. Doll is all original, including roller skates. Marked "Patsykin" on head and "Patsy Jr." on body. In mint condition - **$400.00.** *Courtesy Dale R. Schell.*

In 1937, Effanbee made the composition puppet doll of the famous CHARLIE MCCARTHY. Has cloth body and part of the limbs. The rest is made of composition. All original with pin. Clothes designed by Mollye Goldman. Marked "Edgar Bergan's/Charlie McCarthy/An Effanbee Product." $600.00 up. *Courtesy Joan Guelzov.*

This wonderful HOWDY DOODY was made by Effanbee in 1947. Has composition head, hands, and feet with cloth body and limbs. Sleep eyes are made of glassene. Most of these dolls were 20" tall. All original - $325.00 up. *Courtesy Joan Guelzov.*

21" AMERICAN CHILD designed by Dee Wees Cochron for Effanbee in the 1930s. Made of all latex and composition with painted eyes and closed mouth. Marked "American Child" on head and "Anne Shirley" on back. Shown wearing original clothes and gloves. $1,400.00. *Courtesy Doris Rickert.*

Large 18" Dy-Dee Baby with hard plastic head and rubber body and ears. Shown with cute Dy-Dee diaper pail. Behind her is a 14" Little Lady (Suzanne) in her original case. She was made in 1941. Baby - $185.00 up. Doll with case - $450.00 up. *Courtesy Joan Guelzov.*

Two beautifully mint DyDee Baby dolls from the early 1950s. Both have hard plastic heads, rubber bodies, and caracul wigs. Also shown is a pattern for clothes and a storybook. The larger doll belongs in the original box. 15" - $135.00; 20" - $225.00. *Courtesy Joan Guelzov.*

21" all composition LITTLE LADY with yarn hair and sleep eyes. Made in 1945. In mint, unplayed with condition, shown with original box. Doll only, mint - $525.00. With box - $600.00 up. *Courtesy Martha Sweeney.*

18" all composition HONEY from 1948. This exact doll is shown in the 1948 Montgomery Wards catalog. She also came in 20" to 28" sizes. All original including hat. $500.00 up. *Courtesy Joan Guelzov.*

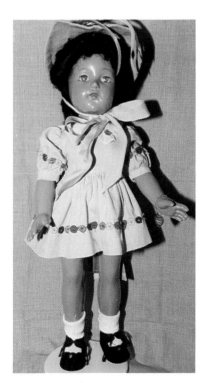

21" extremely rare black LITTLE LADY/ANNE SHIRLEY. Made of all composition with sleep eyes and floss style wig. Marked on head and body. Has coat that matches bonnet. $750.00. *Courtesy Patricia Wood.*

17" HEARTBEAT BABY from 1942 is made of composition and cloth with clockwork mechanism. Turn key to activate heartbeat. Came with stethoscope. $150.00 up. *Courtesy Jeanne Venner.*

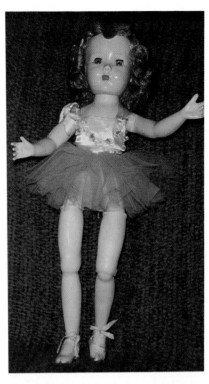

20" HONEY BALLERINA made of all hard plastic with extra joints at knees and ankles. All original except for replaced slippers. $400.00. *Courtesy June Schulz.*

18" and 14" HONEY BRIDESMAIDS made of all hard plastic with closed mouths, sleep eyes, and saran wigs. Both are all original. 18" - $450.00 up. 14" - $325.00 up. *Courtesy Kris Lundquist.*

27" MELODIE made in the 1950s by Effanbee. Has a vinyl head, hard plastic body with jointed knees, and sleep eyes. She talks and sings due to talking mechanism in her back that plays records. For some reason, this particular doll has very thin legs. Most likely, these legs were meant for another doll. Doll is original except for shoes and socks. She is in working order. $300.00. *Courtesy Connie Diehl.*

31" MARY JANE made by Effanbee in 1960. Has vinyl head, rooted hair, and freckles. This is an exceptional example and rarely found. All original. In this condition - $250.00. *Courtesy Susan Girardot.*

15" PATSY ANN representing the Girl Scouts. All vinyl with rooted hair and freckles. All original with wrist tag and in unplayed with condition. $65.00. *Courtesy Susan Girardot.*

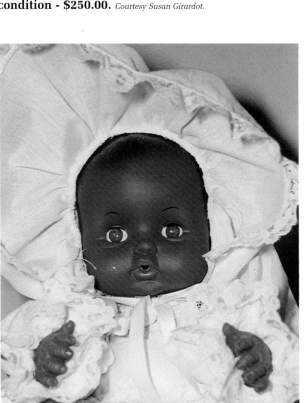

Black BUTTERBALL made of all vinyl with sleep eyes and open mouth/nurser. Made in 1969. $55.00. *Courtesy Kathy Trvdik.*

18" VICTORIAN LADY, #1731, from Effanbee's Grand Dames Series of 1977. Made of plastic and vinyl. $50.00. *Courtesy Pat Graff.*

14½" FALL from Effanbee's Four Seasons Collection of 1983. Made of plastic and vinyl with sleep eyes. $60.00. *Courtesy Pat Graff.*

15½" LOUIS ARMSTRONG has an excellent likeness to the famous entertainer – right down to his diamond ring and hankie. Made by Effanbee in 1984–1985 only. $125.00 up. *Courtesy Margaret Mandel.*

12½" FIRST DATE from the Joyous Occasions Collection. Made of vinyl and plastic with sleep eyes. Marked on head "Z1100/Effanbee/©1988" and on back "Effanbee/ 21300." (Doll's name is NICOLE in the 1989 company catalog.) $75.00. *Courtesy LeeAnn Geary.*

11" INTERNATIONAL USA doll made of plastic and vinyl by Effanbee in 1989–1990. $45.00. *Courtesy Sally Bethschieder.*

18" porcelain dolls from the Eugenia Dukas Collection made by Effanbee in 1988. Both have cloth bodies and painted eyes. Left: LADY NICHOLE, limited edition of 750. $225.00. Right: LADY JACQUELINE, limited edition of 300. $385.00. *Courtesy Pat Graff.*

11" WORLD WAR HERO with movable head and wrists. Action figure has molded-on clothes. Packaging marked "Enjoy your new ELGEE. Made exclusively for Louis Greenberg & Son. NY." $40.00. *Courtesy Randy Numley.*

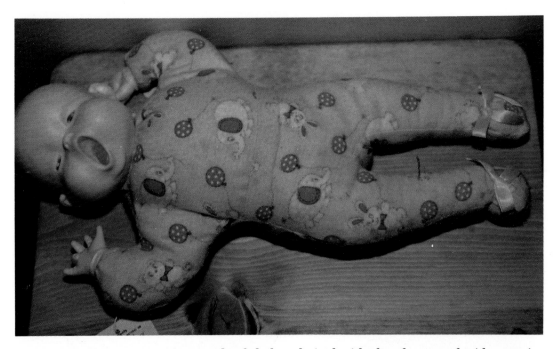

15" YAWNING JOHN or BABY YAWN made of cloth and vinyl with closed eyes and wide yawning mouth. Pajamas form the body and limbs. Has vinyl gaunlet arms. Marked "L-E" on head. Body tagged "By Ellanee Doll Co. 1971." (A 1975 version of the doll can be seen in *Patricia Smith's Doll Values, Volume 10,* page 229.) $45.00. *Courtesy Jeannie Mauldin.*

⁓ Eugenia ⁓

The Eugenia Company originally was the Henry J. Eugene firm located in Jedmunds, England, and their main business was exporting composition dolls in the late 1930s. By 1943, this designer and dollmaker had opened a company in the United States, and like the majority of other dollmakers, could not afford to set up his own factory and had to go to a supplier. He chose Ideal Doll Company to make his line of dolls. He sculpted the head, Ideal made the blanks, and Eugenia dressed and marketed the dolls especially for Montgomery Wards. Wards wanted a doll that was "their own, like Carol Brent," and this doll had a different look. The publicity people at Wards came up with the name "Personality Playmate" for these dolls. Eugenia had two names for the doll — Roberta and Sandra. Roberta was the composition version until 1949, and hard plastic Sandra was made until 1953.

Although a beautiful doll, Roberta and Sandra did not fair well on the market, mainly due to the price. The doll and her clothes were of the finest quality, therefore expensive. Mollye Goldman of Molly-es Doll International purchased the remainder of the dolls after Montgomery Wards declined to purchase another year's supply. There were very few remaining blanks, but they will be found in Molly-e tagged clothes.

Close-up of the Roberta/Sandra head to show detail.

17½" hard plastic SANDRA has a mohair wig and sleep eyes. Gown is tagged and has attached cotton petticoat. This particular doll was most likely dressed and marketed by Molly-e Dolls. $550.00. *Courtesy Pat Graff.*

15" COWGIRL made by Eugenia for Montgomery Wards in 1947. Made of all composition with sleep eyes and mohair wig. Has four painted lashes at upper corners of eyes. All original. $450.00. *Courtesy Elizabeth Montesano.*

22" ELIZABETH ANN made for the K & K Company by Fiberoid. Her happy face has an open mouth and tin sleep eyes. Also has composition head and limbs, swivel neck, and cloth body. Marked "Fiberoid" on shoulderplate. Made in the early 1930s as a competition to Effanbee's ROSEMARY doll and Ideal's pre-Shirley Temple dolls. (Fiberoid was one of the manufacturers that provided made-to-order dolls to doll finishers/marketers.) $400.00. *Courtesy Jeannie Mauldin.*

Redressed 22" doll with composition shoulderhead, tin sleep eyes, and human hair wig. May have originally been black doll or Indian. Marked "Fiberoid" on back shoulder. $400.00. *Courtesy Virginia Sofie.*

☙ Galoob ☙

In 1991, Galoob put out ten different Baby Face dolls – all with a different head, which was a costly thing to do. They were followed in 1992 with seven others along with five babies and one boy. These dolls are of high quality and retail was high. People purchasing dolls for play passed them because of the price. Nobody would buy a child all the dolls.

There are babies, toddlers, and children in this grouping, and it would make a cute collection. Also it would be a challenge to try and locate all of them, along with the variations.

All Baby Face dolls are strung. The babies will have a painted-on shirt like a top, open/closed mouths with moulded tongues, and upper and lower teeth. They will be marked "Galoob. 1990" or "1991 LG TI #20 China." All of the dolls are very detailed in their modeling.

See *Modern Collector Dolls, Volume 6,* pages 117–118 for So Funny Natalie, So Innocent Cynthia, and So Playful Penny. Other characters can be seen in *Patricia Smith's Doll Values, Volume 9,* page 231.

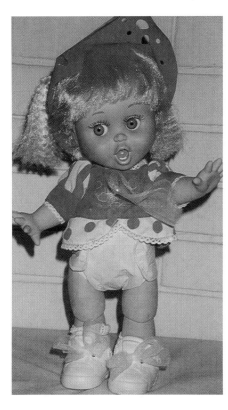

A selection of 13" BABY FACE dolls made by Galoob in 1991. They are made of vinyl with inset eyes and have jointed elbows and knees. All original. Above (left to right): SO SHY SHERRI, SO SURPRISED SUSIE, and SO DELIGHTFUL DEEDEE. Below (left to right): SO LOVELY LAURA, SO SWEET SANDI, and SO SORRY SARAH. Each - $45.00. *Courtesy Pat Graff.*

More 13" BABY FACE dolls made by Galoob in 1991. They are made of vinyl with inset eyes and have jointed elbows and knees. All original. Left to right: TINA, SO HAPPY HEIDI (with open/closed mouth), and CARMEN. Tina, Carmen - $50.00. Heidi - $45.00. *Courtesy Marie Ernst and Pat Graff.*

14" CURIOUS BABY CARA (left) and EXCITED BABY BECCA (right) were made in 1992. They are on strung five-piece bent limb baby bodies made of vinyl with inset eyes. Both are all original. Each - $28.00. *Courtesy Pat Graff.*

14" BASHFUL BABY ABBY was part of the Baby Face collection made by Galoob in 1992. Has all vinyl bent limb baby body and inset eyes. $28.00. *Courtesy Pat Graff.*

14" HAPPY BABY HANNA made of all vinyl with sleep eyes. On five-piece bent limb baby body. Part of Baby Face set of 1992. All original. $28.00. *Courtesy Pat Graff.*

14" SAD BABY BROOKE is part of the Baby Face set from 1992. Made of vinyl with sleep eyes. All original. $28.00. *Courtesy Pat Graff.*

14" SUSIE (SUZY) SNAPSHOT made of rigid vinyl with painted eyes. Has extra joints at wrists and waist. Came with camera, and when camera is aimed at doll's necklace, she changes positions. Made by Galoob in 1990. $50.00. *Courtesy Pat Graff.*

15" FREEDOM KID named KUNG FU. Has cloth body with vinyl head and lower limbs. Silky hair is extra fine, and cheeks have dimples. Head marked "1985 Goodwill International." Wrist tag marked "Passport of the Kingdom of Heaven" and has doll's photo. Inside contains personal details, prayers, and instructions on how doll can perform kung fu. $65.00.

34" LADY LEE made of all hard plastic with sleep eyes and open mouth. All original and in unplayed with condition. Has original box. Although doll is unmarked, box marked "Halso Doll Co." which is the J. Halpern Company that specialized in marketing large 24" and up babies and 27" and up girls/ladies. The large dolls were purchased as blanks from the Paris Doll Co. The babies are from the Horsman Doll Co. In this mint condition - $500.00. *Courtesy Jeannie Mauldin.*

Extremely rare Hartland figure of BILL LONGLEY (RORY CALHOUN) from the TV show, *The Texan.* This program was on television from September 1958 to September 1960. $375.00. *Courtesy Steve Humphries.*

Pony Express horse with mail bags behind saddle. Rider is BUFFALO BILL. Both man and horse are made in one piece, although Bill has a separate hat. $300.00. *Courtesy Steve Humphries.*

Chuck Conners as LUCAS McCAIN in the TV series, *The Rifleman.* $375.00. *Courtesy Steve Humphries.*

≈ Hasbro ≈

Hasbro stands for the name of its founders — the Hassenfeld Brothers. Their main line of business in the 1950s was toys. Even into the 1960s with the GI Joe series, they still considered them toys. Hasbro is most famous for GI Joe, but along the way they developed a few dolls that collectors watch for. Those include

That Kid, a freckled face boy with slingshot from 1967, and the Candy Kids (examples: Babe Ruth, Peppermint Patti, Dots, etc.) The Leggie and World of Love series are sought because they are from the late 1960s and early 1970s, and the fashions from that era are reflected in the doll clothes.

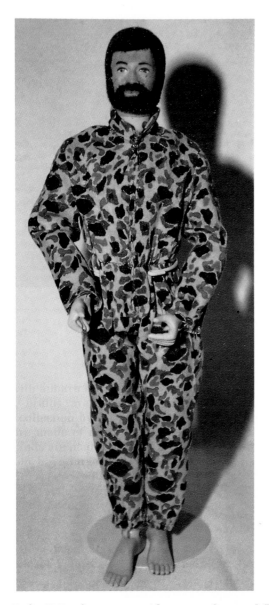

Left: GI JOE from 1964 with scar on face and flocked beard and hair. Dressed in tagged jumpsuit. In this condition - $50.00 up. Right: EAGLE EYE GI JOE with flocked hair, scar on face, and eyes that move from side to side with lever on back of head. Clothes are not original. Mint - $125.00.

18" AIMEE by Hasbro in 1972. She has a very unique character doll design. Made of vinyl with rooted hair. She had many extra outfits available. The one on the right is made of all velvet. Each - $50.00. *Courtesy Marie Ernst.*

9½" SOUL of the World of Love Doll series. This set also included LOVE, PEACE, FLOWER, and MUSIC. They had bendable knees and jointed waists. (Another SOUL can be seen in *Modern Collector's Dolls*, Volume 1, page 133 in a different outfit.) $15.00. *Courtesy Kathy Trvdik.*

12" GLITTER 'N GOLD JEM with blonde/gold hair and lavender eyes. Legs can cross. Has white skirt to take place of gold outfit to become a business suit. $75.00. *Courtesy Claudia Meeker.*

This shows all the fashions in JEM's Glitter 'n Gold collection. All are shown except "Morroccan Magic" (top right.) Each - $20.00. *Courtesy Claudia Meeker.*

"Midnight Magic" from 1986. $20.00.
Courtesy Claudia Meeker.

"Gold Rush" from 1986. $20.00.
Courtesy Claudia Meeker.

"Golden Days, Diamond Nights" from 1986. $20.00.
Courtesy Claudia Meeker.

"Purple Haze" from the JEM's Glitter 'n Gold fashion collection of 1986. $20.00. *Courtesy Claudia Meeker.*

"Fire & Ice" from the Glitter 'n Gold fashions, 1986. $20.00. *Courtesy Claudia Meeker.*

12" ROCK & CURL JEM from 1986. Came with can of hair spray and hair could be styled in many ways. Hair flows from white to pink. (Also see *Modern Collector's Dolls, Volume 6*, pg. 125 for better photo.) $50.00. *Courtesy Claudia Meeker.*

Left: 12½" CLASH OF THE MISFITS, rival rock group of JEM & THE HOLOGRAMS. She has purple paint under rooted purple hair, very pale pink lips, and blue patch over one painted blue eye. Also has extra joints at wrist, waist, and knees. Comes with cassette, headphones, and "distortion modulator." Right: Back of the MISFITS box shows STORMER (blue hair), ROSY (white hair), CLASH (purple hair), and PIZZAZ (yellow hair.) Each - $50.00. *Courtesy Claudia Meeker.*

This separate outfit box shows the clothes from the Flip Side Fashions collection designed for JEM IN 1986. All are shown except "Let's Rock This Town," "Rock Country," and "Gettin' Down To Business." Each - $15.00–20.00. *Courtesy Claudia Meeker.*

"Up 'n Rockin'" from JEM's Flip Side Fashions. $15.00. *Courtesy Claudia Meeker.*

"Like A Dream" from Flip Side Fashions. $15.00. *Courtesy Claudia Meeker.*

"Music in the Air" from Flip Side Fashions. $15.00. *Courtesy Claudia Meeker.*

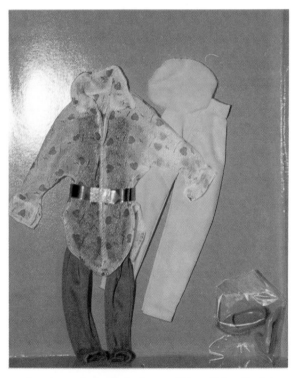

"Sophisticated Lady" from Flip Side Fashions. $18.00. *Courtesy Claudia Meeker.*

"City Lights" from the Flip Side Fashions collection. $15.00. *Courtesy Claudia Meeker.*

12" FLASH 'N SIZZLE JEM/JERRICA with bendable knees and jointed at waist and wrists. Has two A-76 cell batteries to operate flashing earrings. Comes with pink/yellow JERRICA daytime outfit. $45.00. *Courtesy Claudia Meeker.*

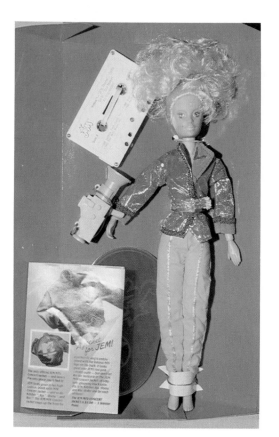

Left: 12" VIDEO OF THE HOLOGRAMS from 1986. Has purple eye color around blue painted eyes and beauty mark. Comes with video camera and mail-in offer for MTV jacket ($3.00 + one Jemstar point printed on the package.) Right: Box back shows the music force behind JEM — the HOLOGRAMS. Only one of them knows her true identity. Their names are KIMBER, AGA, SHANA, RAJA, and DANSE, the choreographer (holding radio.) Each - $45.00. *Courtesy Claudia Meeker.*

In 1987, Hasbro introduced the STARLIGHT GIRLS, who were JERRICA'S friends living at the Starlight House. These 11" dolls had soft vinyl arms, bendable knees with good knee detail, and extra joints at waist only. On the left is KRISSIE and on the right is BANEE with long black hair. Blonde ASHLEY is shown on the box. They are marked "1987 Hasbro, Inc./Made in Hong Kong/All Rights Reserved." In box - $30.00. Doll only - $18.00.

☞ Himstedt ☜

The following Himstedt information has been compiled by Carmen Holshoe, a dedicated collector, and the author. We are admirers of Annette Himstedt's ability to capture children's expressions in her life-like doll creations.

The author also wants to thank the following people who gave of their time and expertise to help make this section successful: Geri Cote,

Joan Kontoes of Joan's Treasured Dolls (337 Central Street, Franklin, NH 03243), and Diane Camden of Camden House, Inc. (3414 Noble Road, Richmond, VA 23222. Telephone: 800-834-2911.) Written information was obtained from *Dolls – The Collector's Magazine*, *Doll Reader Magazine*, and brochures enclosed with Himstedt dolls.

This section is dedicated to a very beautiful and sweet child, Chelsey Holshoe, age 11, shown holding her favorite Himstedt, ANNCHEN.

Annette Himstedt is a young sculptress from Paderbron, Germany, and a self-taught artist who has been creating her own unique style since 1979. She was once an insurance salesperson who taught herself how to model doll heads and limbs from porcelain. Himstedt has stated, "When I was a child, I did not have any dolls," but she loved to paint portraits and later moved on to sculpting. Her first dolls, made in 1975, were constructed of stone and cloth, but she progressed to working with porcelain in 1979, the medium she uses today. Himstedt said, "Sculpting — it's my life. I sculpt in the evening and on the weekends." A 14-hour day is not uncommon for her. She is very dedicated to her work, and through this dedication, she has built her self-confidence and the ability to assert herself in a strong, positive way. This form of independence plays a very important part in her life and allows her to be able to balance her work and travel schedules. While she travels, it is not unusual for her to see a child whose face captures her imagination. It will be a face that expresses

something special, and she will ask the parents to allow her to photograph the child.

Annette Himstedt surprised everyone with her first lifelike porcelain doll, modeled after her own daughter, Lisa. Because this doll became so popular with everyone who saw it, she was soon making other lifelike porcelain dolls of the the neighborhood children. Each were modeled and scaled to perfection after a real child.

The true-to-life quality of all Himstedt dolls have fooled a few people who have walked into a room, slightly glanced at a doll, and greeted it as if it was a child — leaving that person embarrassed and looking around to see if anyone saw them. Generally, these people start to collect every Himstedt doll they can find. Their unique and impeccable artistry make these dolls very desirable for any collection.

From one of her first booklets, Ms. Himstedt stated, "When I first started to make dolls, everyone told me that everything I wanted to do was impossible. I have always done what I wanted to do. I have always believed things to be possible which others thought were impossible. No one has been able to stop me from continuing." This shows the very strong personality that it takes to become successful.

By 1982, Himstedt was selling one-of-a-kind dolls from a department store in Munich, Germany. She continued these unique porcelains and also added limited edition porcelains at the rate of six or seven a year. Due to the emphasis on details, it takes approximately one year to complete one Himstedt doll.

In 1985, Himstedt sculpted and developed two dolls in vinyl, Fatou and Bekus, which were shown at the Nurenburg Toy Fair. Fatou is also called Corn Row Fatou because her human hair is styled in corn row braids. Fatou is limited to 81 pieces and has glass eyes and dark skin. Bekus is a boy doll from Nepal, a country in the Himalaya Mountains. He also has dark skin, human hair, and glass eyes. When Mattel Toy Co. saw the innovative style of these dolls and realized their sales potential in the United State, they contracted with Ms. Himstedt to be her distributor.

Overcoming all problems and working many 12 to 14 hour days, Himstedt went to Spain where she leased a factory to make her first vinyl series, The Barefoot Children, which were the first Himstedt dolls available to American collectors. A point of interest: Mattel is the United States marketing distributor. They do not see the dolls, which are shipped directly to the shops from Spain. Ms. Himstedt's porcelain dolls come directly from Paderborn, Germany.

Annette Himstedt is personally involved in every single stage of development and production – from the rough sketches to the last creative detail, such as using real hair for wigs and eyelashes. She inspects every step and detail, including the hand painting, the positioning of the eyes, and the quality of the hand knotted wigs. All her dolls leave the factory looking exactly like her originals. Ms. Himstedt and the people in her workshop bring to completion what her mind has conceived and her hands have developed. The child-like realism

sparkles in the eyes of each and every doll Himstedt manufactures.

Himstedt has engraved all the important facts for collectors on the back of each doll's head. An original doll bears her signature, the year it was made, Germany (the country of origin), the name of the doll, Annette Himstedt's name, and copyright. Her name is also engraved on each limb to make forgeries impossible. Each article of clothing — dress, pinafore, slip, and slacks — are tagged with the Himstedt signature. Each doll comes with a certificate of authenticity and a registration card. The first series of the Barefoot Children will be marked West Germany instead of Germany.

Ms. Himstedt is so precise that it can take her up to 400 hours to finish a face. There are up to 60 coats of glaze applied to the porcelains to create the life-like tones of the heads, and the limbs will have from 10 to 12 coats of glaze. The porcelains take from 10 to 20 kiln firings at 2,642° F. The eyes are mouth blown glass, the wigs are hand done, and the dresses are made from antique fabrics and laces. A professional shoemaker makes the shoes. If any beading is required for the costume, it is done by hand.

The simple outfit worn by Barefoot Child Bastian is an example of detail. His pants are lined of the same fabric as his shirt and button-on suspenders. The coordination of fabrics to create costumes reflecting an area or country is simple yet very detailed. Details such as buttons, undergarments, pinafores trimmed with embroidered, scalloped edged eyelet are all special touches by this artist. In order to create the open/closed mouth used for the Lisa and Kasimer dolls, a special molding process with extra handwork was required. Everything about an Annette Himstedt doll is special — right down to the clothing being woven from the finest natural fibers and the personalized labels sewn into each garment as a finishing touch of the artist.

In 1986, personal signatures by the artist started with the first "signing party" of the Barefoot Child Fatou, also known as the

American Fatou. The artist's appearance and signing was held at FAO Schwarz and the dolls were autographed with a red pen, depicting the Schwarz colors of red on white. Any dolls autographed by the artist after that date were signed with a gold metallic pen. Due to the nature of the gold pen, many autographs have turned green. It is also known that autographs may fade over the years. Dolls are signed on the back shoulderplate, and on babies, the bottom of the foot.

On the subject of mold sales, Himstedt states, "I have never sold my molds and will not do so in the future." This is *extremely important*, as many doll artists are selling their molds to mold companies or selling them themselves. This causes the immediate decline in doll value and decreased desirability for that artist's work. Buyers do not know if they have an original or one made by the lady across town. This practice has further mudded the already murky waters of the doll artist market over the past 10 years, especially for anyone interested in documenting the dolls for publication.

Annette Himstedt has only been in the American doll artist arena for 10 years, but what an impact she has made! The combination of this artist's unique styling, creativity, and realism bring her doll children to life. That rare sensitivity to life has made – and will continue to make – Himstedt dolls so desirable and appealing to collectors from around the world.

Guide to Annette Himstedt Dolls

Pre-Mattel, Inc. Dolls

Name	Date	Country Represented	Issue	Value
Cornrow Fatou (Called big-eyed Fatou)	1985	Africa	60 For Nuenberg Toy Fair	$2,500.00
Cornrow Fatou (Face mold was refined for the American market)	late 1985	Africa	81	$1,600.00–1,800.00
Bekus	1985	Nepal	60	$2,200.00
Bekus, big eyed	1985	Nepal	60 For Nuenberg Toy Fair	$2,200.00
Bastian, big eyed Longer hair, brown corduroy overalls, white striped shirt	1985	Nepal	60	$2,400.00

Ellen, Paula, Kathe, and Lisa with Big Eyes, made in 1985 for the Toy Fair, have wonderful face coloring and were not made in Spain, but in a factory in Germany for the European market. The American Paula may be a little pale.

Name	Market	Issue	Value
Ellen with big eyes	made for Europe	60	$1,500.00
Paula with big eyes	made for Europe	60	$1,800.00

Name	Market	Issue	Value
Kathe with big eyes	made for Europe	60	$1,800.00
Lisa with big eyes (in plain all blue dress)		60	$2,400.00
Lisa (in blue with embroidered vest)		60	$1,800.00
Same face mold as the American Lisa			

Distributed by Mattel, Inc.
Shipped directly from Spain to the United States

Please note: Prices for vinyl and porcelain dolls are estimated current values taken from known selling prices, both from dealer to collector and collector to collector. Variations of prices may happen from area to area.

The prices shown are based on a mint-in-box doll with all certificates correctly numbered to the doll. If vinyl, all limbs are impressed with Himstedt name. If doll has been personally autographed by Annette Himstedt, add an additional $150.00–200.00 to price.

The Barefoot Children Series

Name	Size	Year	Country	Retail	Current
Bastian	26"	1986	Germany	$300.00	$850.00
Ellen	26"	1986	Germany	$300.00	$900.00
Kathe	26"	1986	Germany	$300.00	$900.00
Paula	26"	1986	Germany	$300.00	$800.00
Lisa*	26"	1986	Germany	$300.00	$900.00 up
Fatou**	26"	1986	Germany	$300.00	$1,000.00

* Lisa is a portrait of Annette Himstedt's daughter at age 5. The German version of Lisa will have on a blue dress; the American version will be wearing a red and white striped dress with pinafore. Allow more for the blue dress (hard to find). Lisa has a smiling open/closed mouth showing upper and lower teeth.

** This Fatou is also called the American Fatou and was used at the first signing party by Annette Himstedt at the FAO Schwarz store. She wears a rust colored dress with white pinafore and has dark skin.

The American Heartland Series (Prairie Children)

Name	Size	Year	Country	Retail	Current
Toni	23"	1987	America	$300.00	$600.00
Timi	21"	1987	America	$300.00	$650.00

World Children Series

Name	Size	Year	Country	Retail	Current
Michiko	30"	1988	Japan	$500.00	$1,300.00
Makimura	30"	1988	Japan	$500.00	$1,200.00
Malin	30"	1988	Sweden	$500.00	$1,650.00
Friederike	30"	1988	Hungry	$500.00	$1,800.00
Kasimir*	30"	1988	Germany	$500.00	$1,850.00–2,100.00

* Kasimir has a smiling, open/closed mouth with upper and lower teeth.

Reflection of Youth Series

Name	Size	Year	Country	Retail	Current
Janka	26"	1989	Hungary	$550.00	$900.00
Adrienne*	26"	1989	France	$600.00	$900.00
Ayoka**	26"	1989	Africa	$600.00	$1,200.00
Kai***	26"	1989	Germany	$600.00	$900.00

* Adrienne won the D.O.T.Y. (Doll of the Year) Award in 1989.
** Ayoka has approximately 45+ beads in her human hair braided wig, triple row beaded necklace, two beaded bracelets, and one beaded ankle bracelet. There are two earrings in left ear and one in right ear.
*** Kai has an earring in left ear, wears shorts and knee socks, and has sneakers that are impressed on the sole with the Himstedt signature.

Fiene and The Barefoot Babies Series

Name	Size	Year	Country	Retail	Current
Fiene*	28"	1990	Belguim	$600.00	$900.00
Mo**	22"	1990	USA	$450.00	$800.00
Taki**	22"	1990	Japan	$450.00	$1,100.00
Annchen**	22"	1990	Germany	$450.00	$850.00

* Fiene won the Doll Face of the Year Award in 1990.
** All babies have beads in a cloth body. Every so often, take your doll and tip it upside down to redistribute the beads. If not, the beads may settle to the bottom of the doll.

Faces of Friendship Series

Name	Size	Year	Country	Retail	Current
Shireem	28"	1991	Bali	$550.00	$650.00
Liliane	28"	1991	Netherlands	$550.00	$800.00
Neblina	28"	1991	Switzerland	$550.00	$700.00

Summer Dreams Series

Name	Size	Year	Locale	Retail	Current
Enzo	26"	1992	Italy	$550.00	$550.00
Pemba	23"	1992	Alabama	$550.00	$550.00
Sanga*	23"	1992	Tennessee	$550.00	$600.00
Jule	23"	1992	Sweden	$550.00	$700.00

* Sanga won the 1992 Dolls Award of Excellence in vinyl.

Images of Childhood Series

Name	Size	Year	Locale	Retail	Current
Tara	28"	1993	Germany	$600.00	$600.00
Lona	29"	1993	California	$600.00	$600.00
Kima*	27"	1993	Greenland	$600.00	$700.00

* Kima won Dolls of Excellence Award, Doll of the Year Award, and Doll Face of the Year Award.

Children Together Series

Name	Size	Year	Country	Retail	Current
Panchita*	27"	1994	Mexico	$599.00	$500.00
Poncho	28"	1994	Mexico	$599.00	$500.00
Alke	28"	1994	Norway	$599.00	$500.00
Melvin**	30"	1994	England	$599.00	$500.00

* Panchita won the Doll Face of the Year Award in 1994.
** The first Melvins have short hair to the ear lobes and very short eyelashes. The second version has hair to shoulders and very long eyelashes. Panchita, Poncho, and Melvin have straight legs.

Decade of Children of The World Series

Annette Himstedt is celebrating a decade of dolls in the United States and the following are the 10th anniversary collection. Each anniversary doll wears a special bracelet.

Name	Size	Year	Locale	Retail	Current
Minou*	29"	1995	Corsica	$599.00	$599.00
Madina	28"	1995	Russia	$599.00	$599.00
Takuma**	26"	1995	Cheyenne	$599.00	$599.00
Takumi**	26"	1995	Cheyenne	$599.00	$599.00

* Minou's wig is mohair
** Annette Himstedt's first set of twins.

Porcelain Dolls

Porcelain dolls have been available in the United States since 1990, and these excellent early Annette Himstedt creations were distributed by European Artists Dolls. In February 1993, full-page advertisements appeared, announcing "Beginning with the 1993 collection, all porcelain dolls will be distributed by myself under the name of Kinder aus Porzellan."

It is certain that every porcelain Himstedt doll will be a treasure forever – handed down from generation to generation. They are also limited editions with fewer than 100 worldwide. A few have already become rare treasures.

Each porcelain doll comes in a beige box with a drawing of the doll on the cover. Inside is a sturdy type foam that has been formed to the size of the doll. Each part of the doll – head, limbs, and body – are tied with pieces of fabric tape. Another piece of formed foam is placed on top of the doll. The packing is the best possible and insures the doll will arrive without breakage from Germany. Each doll comes with a signed, numbered certificate. The doll is also signed and numbered on the back of the neck with Annette Himstedt's signature in gold. Even the shipping carton will have Ms. Himstedt's name, studio address, the doll's name, and the number of the doll on it. If current values are marked (*), the current values are not known, as owners will not sell.

World Child Collection

Name	Size	Year	Type or Style	Edition	Retail	Current
Fee	26"	1990	Little girl	80	$3,900.00	$5,800.00
Ruki	24"	1990	Baby boy	80	$3,650.00	$6,000.00
Sita	26"	1990	Gypsy girl	80	$5,000.00	$5,200.00

Children Out Of Porcelain Series

Name	Size	Year	Type or Style	Edition	Retail	Current
Tatum	27"	1991	Eurasian	95	$4,650.00	$5,500.00
Sanseari	27"	1991	Apache girl	95	$5,500.00	$7,500.00
Tatanka	27"	1991	Apache boy	95	$5,700.00	$7,500.00
Leesa	24"	1991	Blonde girl	90	$4,500.00	$4,800.00
Ontje	28"	1991	Auburn boy	90	$4,200.00	$5,000.00
Sam	29"	1991	Red-haired boy	90	$4,600.00	$4,900.00

Fantasy Children

Name	Size	Year	Type or Style	Edition	Retail	Current
Afrika	25"	1992	Boy	90	$5,500.00	$8,500.00

Name	Size	Year	Type or Style	Edition	Retail	Current
Afrika	22"	1992	Girl	90	$5,500.00	$8,500.00
Lill*	26"	1992	Green hair	90	$5,600.00	$5,600.00
Jill*	28"	1992	Pink hair	90	$5,600.00	$5,600.00
Ming	23"	1992	Oriental	90	$4,800.00	$4,800.00
Ling	23"	1992	Oriental	90	$4,800.00	$4,800.00

* Lill and Jill are also known as the Schwestern Pair.

Kinder Aus Porzellan – 1993

Name	Size	Year	Type or Style	Edition	Retail	Current
Mohini*	28"	1993	Indian (country) girl	80	$5,250.00	$7,500.00
Mohan	29"	1993	Indian (country) boy	80	$5,250.00	$7,500.00
Arana**	?	1993	Gypsy girl	25	$6,900.00	$7,200.00
Dragan**	?	1993	Gypsy boy	25	$6,500.00	$7,200.00
Annabella	26"	1993	Girl in blue	90	$3,100.00	$3,400.00
Isa-Belita	28"	1993	Girl in white	90	$4,150.00	$4,150.00*
Nanja	23"	1993	Red hair	90	$3,400.00	$3,800.00
Marie-Claire	28"	1993	Girl with bow	90	$4,600.00	$5,200.00

* Mohini was nominated for Doll Award of Excellence at the American International Toy Fair in New York City, February 8, 1993.
** Reportedly only seven of each doll came to United States.

Kinder Aus Porzellan – 1994

Name	Size	Year	Type or Style	Edition	Retail	Current
Latie	27"	1994	Tibetian girl	80	$6,100.00	$6,400.00
Dalanar	29"	1994	Tibetian boy	80	$5,600.00	$6,000.00
Serita	29"	1994	Indian (country) girl	70	$7,500.00	$8,000.00
Ondal	29"	1994	Indian (country) boy	70	$7,500.00	$8,000.00
Mela	26"	1994	Irish girl	90	$2,800.00	$2,800.00*
Luka	26"	1994	Irish boy	90	$3,100.00	$3,100.00*
Blanda	28"	1994	Griechenland	80	$4,100.00	$4,400.00
Auschra*	?	1994	Madchen girl	25	$8,000.00	$8,600.00
Florinda*	?	1994	Memelland	25	$8,000.00	$8,600.00

* Auschra and Florinda were sold out immediately. Auschra has blonde hair and Florinda is a redhead. Both wear large brimmed hats.

Kinder Aus Porzellan – 1995

Name	Size	Year	Type or Style	Edition	Retail	Current
Jolande*	?	1995	Land of Fairies	25	?	
Jorinde*	?	1995	Land of Fairies	25	?	
Shiangi	?	1995	Chinese girl	70	?	
Mel Li	?	1995	Chinese girl	70	?	
Mayuki	?	1995	Africa	80	$6,500.00	$6,500.00
Kajali	?	1995	Africa	80	$6,500.00	$6,500.00
Linne	?	1995	Sweden	90	?	
Lisbeth	?	1995	Sweden	90	?	
Lasse	?	1995	Sweden	90	?	

* Jolande and Jorinde from the Land of Fairies sold out immediately.

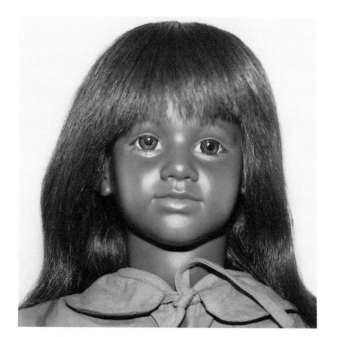 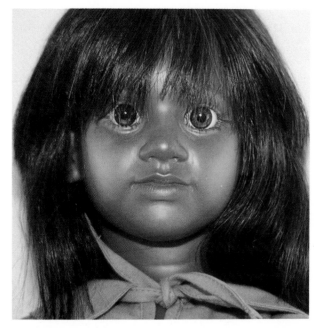

Left: 25" BEKUS made for the German market in 1985. Shown at the Nurenberg Toy Fair. Only 60 dolls were made and all documents included with doll are printed in German. Right: "Big eyed" BEKUS. *Courtesy Carmen Holshoe and Diane Camden.*

 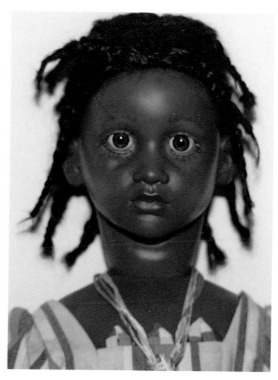

On the left is CORNROW FATOU with regular eyes; on the right, big-eyed CORNROW FATOU. *Courtesy Diane Camden.*

Left: Big-eyed BASTIAN. *Courtesy Diane Camden.*

Below center: 25" BASTIAN from 1986 that was made for German market. (See difference to the American model.) *Courtesy Annette Himstedt.*

Below right: 26" BASTIAN from Barefoot Children Series of 1986. *Courtesy Carmen Holshoe.*

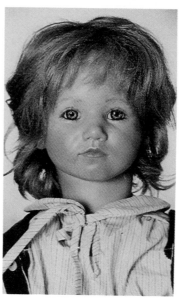 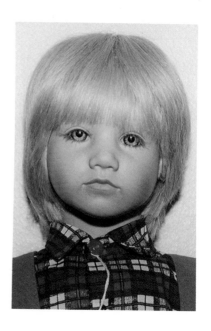

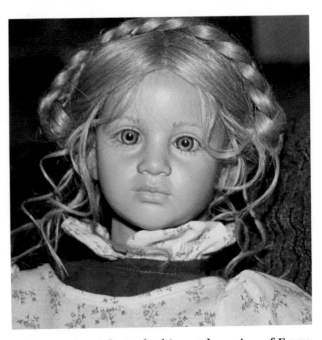

On the left is 26" Ellen of the Barefoot Children of 1986. On the right is the big-eyed version of Ellen.

Courtesy Carmen Holshoe and Diane Camden.

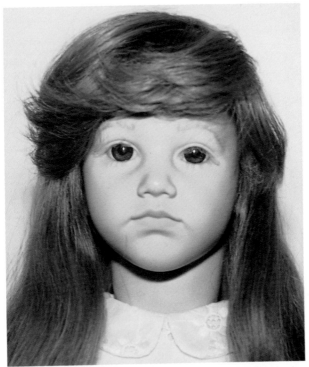

Left: 26" Paula of the Barefoot Children Series of 1986. Right: Big-eyed version of Paula. Hair has been braided and floral coronet has been added. *Courtesy Carmen Holshoe and Diane Camden.*

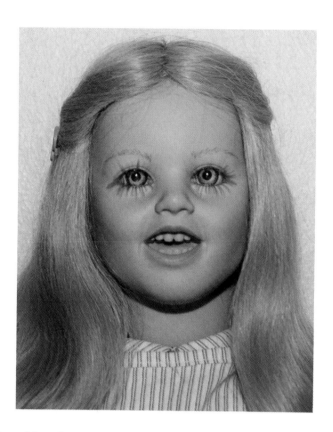

26" LISA was the first of two dolls made with an open/closed laughing mouth. She was a part of the Barefoot Children Series from 1986. Upper right is LISA made for Germany. Note inset eyelashes in bottom left. Lower right shows her limbs and dress. Has cloth body. (LISA is a portrait of Annette Himstedt's daughter at age 5.) *Courtesy Carmen Holshoe.*

26" FATOU made for the United States in 1986. The one made for Germany is dressed in all ivory white dress and considered by many to be the most beautiful doll in the series. *Courtesy Carmen Holshoe.*

26" KATHE who is the pouty in the Barefoot Children Series of 1986. She has cloth body and vinyl limbs. *Courtesy Carmen Holshoe.*

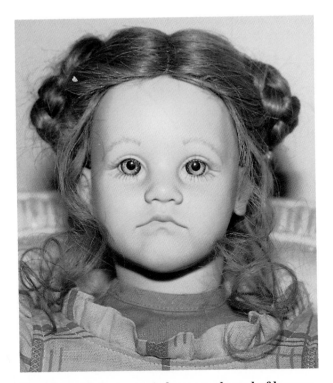

KATHE'S red hair is carried over to the red of her eyelashes. Her pouty mouth gives an unhappy expression to her eyes. *Courtesy Carmen Holshoe.*

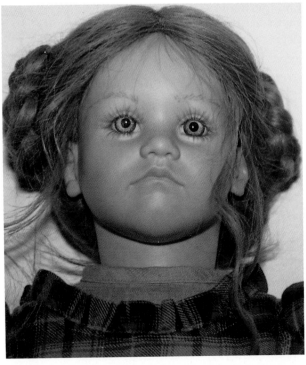

German, but not big-eyed, KATHE with plaid dress. *Courtesy Diane Camden.*

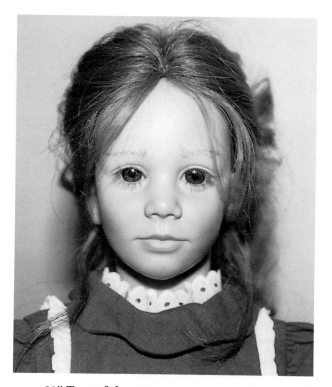 

23" TONI of the 1987 American Heartland Series. On the right is the German version. *Courtesy Carmen Holshoe.*

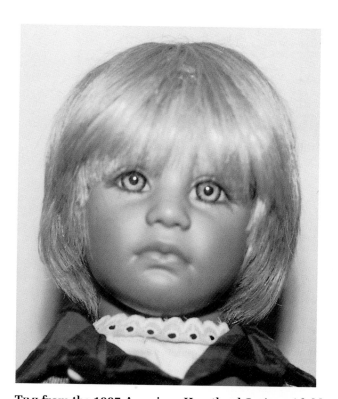 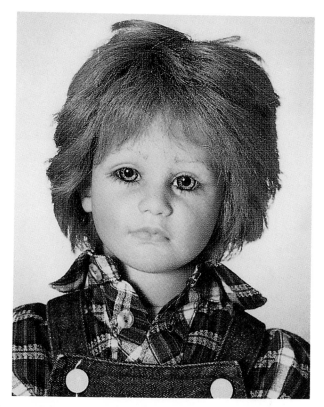

TIMI from the 1987 American Heartland Series with blond hair and faded overalls. On the right is the German version. *Courtesy Carmen Holshoe.*

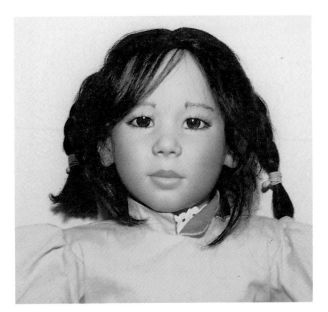

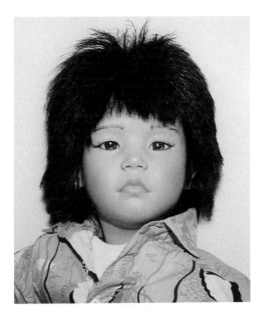

30" MICHIKO (left) and MAKIMURA (right) from the World of Children Series from 1988. They depict Japanese children. *Courtesy Carmen Holshoe.*

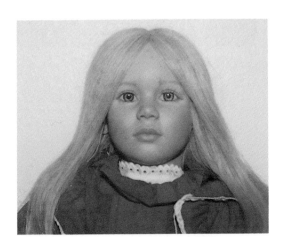

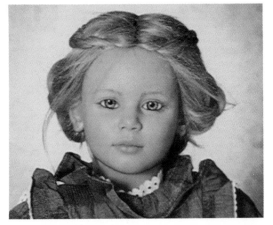

Left: 30" MALIN of Sweden is a part of the World Children Series of 1988. Right: The German version MALIN has different hairdo and dress. *Courtesy Carmen Holshoe.*

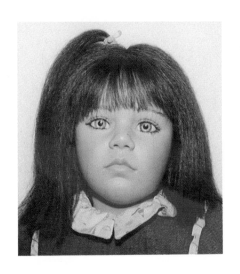

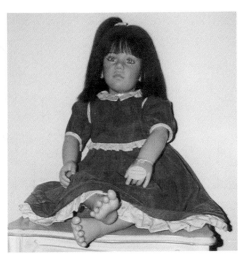

30" FREDERIKA from 1988 World Children Series.

Courtesy Carmen Holshoe.

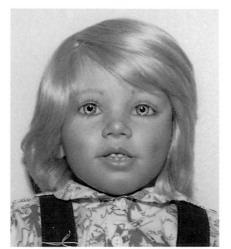

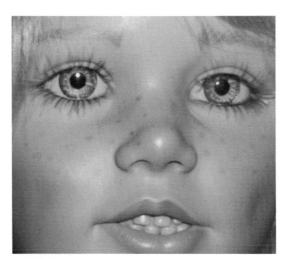

30" KASIMER with side swept hairdo, cheek dimples, freckles, open/closed mouth, and two rows of teeth. Note insert lashes. From 1988.
Courtesy Carmen Holshoe.

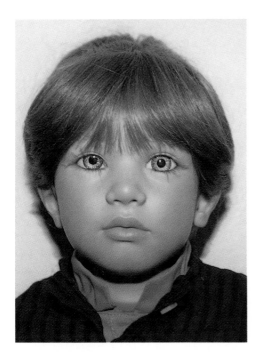

26" JANKA from the 1989 Reflections of Youth Series. She represents a girl from Hungary. *Courtesy Carmen Holshoe.*

26" ADRIENNE from the Reflections of Youth Series of 1989. She represents a girl from France. She won the D.O.T.Y. (Doll of the Year) Award. *Courtesy Carmen Holshoe.*

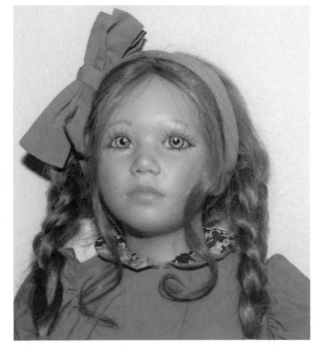

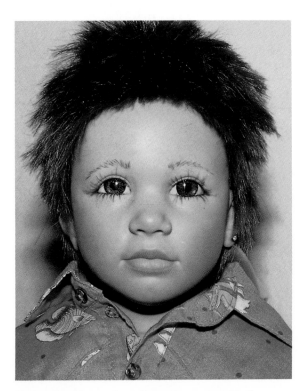

26" KAI from the 1989 Reflections of Youth Series. He is a boy from Germany. He has earring in his left ear and wears sneakers with the Himstedt signature. *Courtesy Carmen Holshoe.*

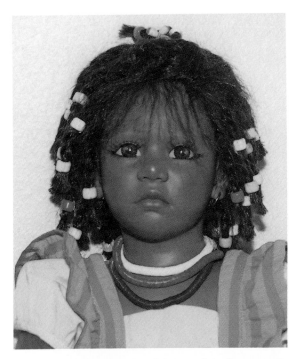

26" AYOKA represents Africa and is from 1989. Her hair is braided with about 45 beads. She has three beaded necklaces, two beaded bracelets, and an ankle bracelet. She also has two earrings in left ear and one in right. *Courtesy Carmen Holshoe.*

28" FIENE is a Belgium child and is part of the Fiene and the Barefoot Babies Series. Dolls sold in Europe have red hair. Her face won the Doll Face of the Year Award in 1990. *Courtesy Carmen Holshoe.*

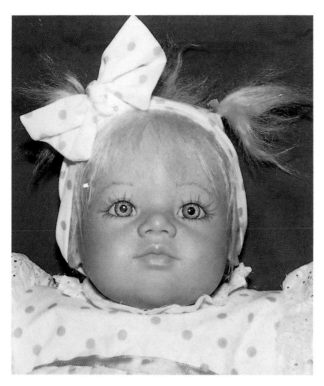

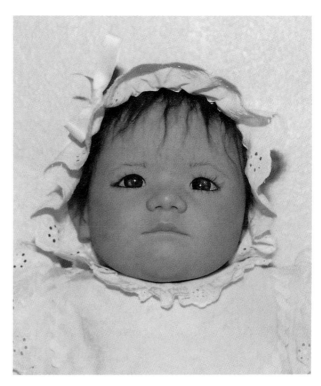

Two babies from the Fiene and the Barefoot Babies Series of 1990. Left: 22" ANNCHEN is a German baby with near white hair and large blue eyes. Right: 22" TAKI is a Japanese baby. *Courtesy Chelsey and Carmen Holshoe.*

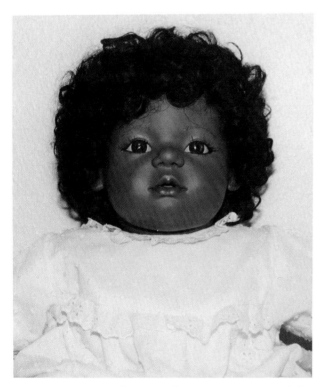

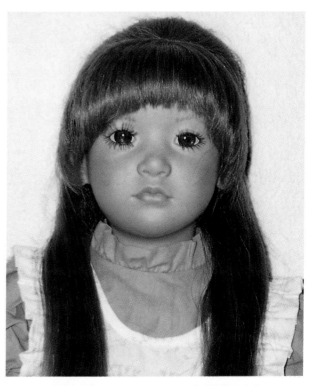

22" MO represents the United States in Fiene and the Barefoot Babies Series from 1990. *Courtesy Carmen Holshoe.*

28" NEBLINA represents a Swiss child from the Faces of Friendship Series of 1991. *Courtesy Geri Cote.*

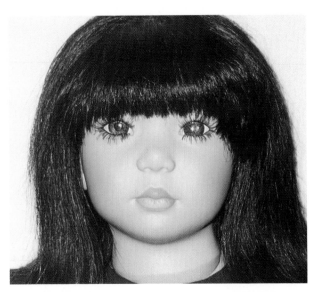

28" SHIREEM of the 1991 Faces of Friendship Series. She is a girl from Bali. *Courtesy Geri Cote.*

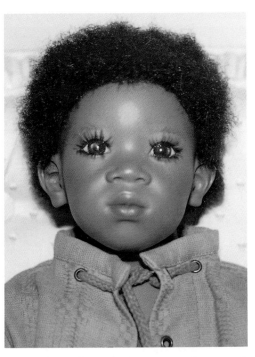

23" PEMBA from the 1992 Summer Dreams Series. Represents a boy from Alabama. *Courtesy Carmen Holshoe.*

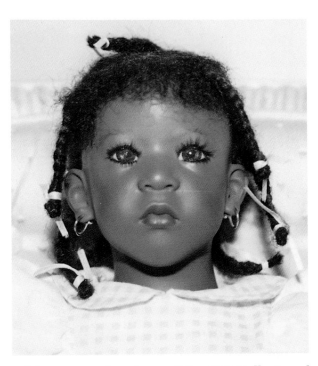

23" SANGA was the winner of the 1990 Dolls Award of Excellence in vinyl. She is from the Summer Dreams Series and represents a girl from Tennessee.

Courtesy Carmen Holshoe.

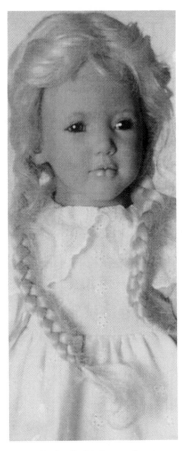

23" JULE is a Swedish child from the Summer Dreams Series of 1992. *Courtesy Himstedt advertisement.*

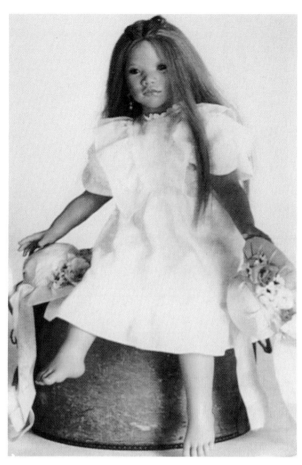

28" TARA is a German girl from the 1993 Images of Childhood Series. *Courtesy advertisement copy.*

29" LONA represents a California child. She is part of the 1993 Images of Childhood Series. *Courtesy advertisement copy.*

27" KIMA from the 1993 Images of Childhood Series is representing Greenland. Received the Doll of Excellence Award, Doll of the Year Award, and Doll Face of the Year Award. *Courtesy Carmen Holshoe.*

27" PANCHITA is a Mexican child from the 1994 Children Together Series. She won the Doll Face of the Year Award. *Courtesy Carmen Holshoe.*

28" ALKE is a Norwegian child in the 1994 Children Together Series. *Courtesy Joan's Treasured Dolls.*

The very first MELVIN dolls have hair to the ear lobes and very short eyelashes. The second version has hair to the shoulders and very long eyelashes. Also there is a difference in face shape and the pants are longer on the second version. Left is Geri Cotes and right is Joan Kontoes. *Courtesy Joan's Treasured Dolls.*

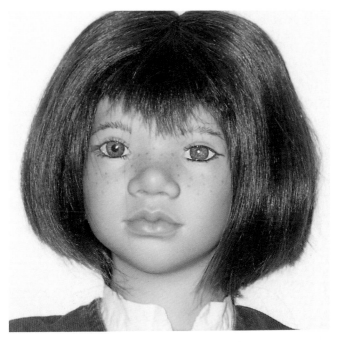

30" MELVIN from the 1994 Children Together Series represents an English boy. He has freckles and stands very well. *Courtesy Carmen Holshoe.*

This advertisement appeared during 1994 in American magazines and was sponsored by Mattel, Inc. Timeless Creations. Hopefully not too many collectors purchased counterfeit dolls. This ad spurred on a heavy buying of the real MELVIN doll.

Top left: MINOU of Corsica is one of the 10th Anniversary Collection. Top right: MADINA from Russia. Sitting: TAKUMA and TAKUMI are Cheyenne Indian twins. Each wears a limited edition bracelet that reads "10 Years Annette Himstedt Puppen Kinder." Distributed by Mattel Inc. (Timeless Creations) in United States. *Courtesy Himstedt advertisement.*

27" SANSEARI is a very authenic Apache girl with excellent details such as the beading, feathers, and leather boots which are sewn together with leather strips. The doll's quality has to be seen to be fully appreciated! Limited to 95 dolls and is a part of the Children Out of Porcelain Series of 1991. *Courtesy Himstedt advertisement and Carmen Holshoe.*

27" TATANKA is an Apache boy dressed in an extremely fine detailed costume which includes beading, leather, and feathers. He is barefoot with fantastic toe detail. This child is part of the Children Out of Porcelain Series of 1991 and is limited to 95 dolls. *Courtesy Carmen Holshoe.*

27" TATUM is a porcelain Eurasian girl from the 1991 Children Out of Porcelain Series. Limited to 95 pieces.

Courtesy Himstedt advertisement.

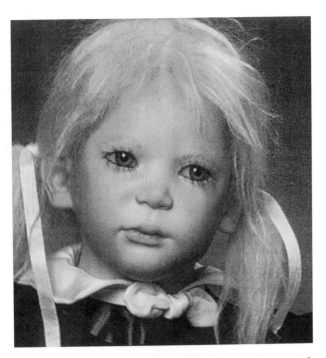

Dolls from the 1991 Children Out of Porcelain Series – 29" SAM (top left), 24" LEESA (top right), 28" ONTJE with auburn hair (lower left). All are limited to 90 pieces. *Courtesy Himstedt advertisement.*

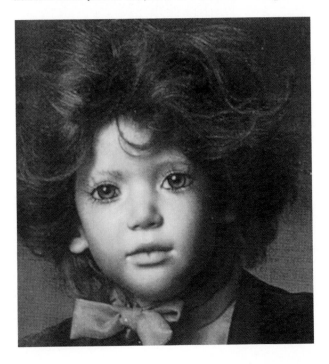

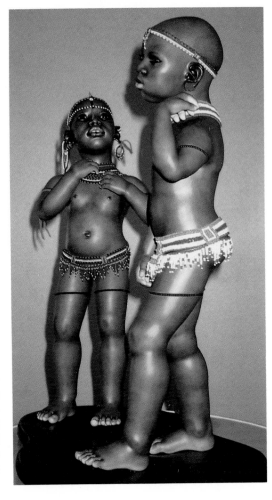

22" and 25" AFRIKA boy and girl made in 1992 as part of the Fantasy Children collection. Limited to 90 each. These dolls are so realistic and detailed that they will one day be considered fine art and be found in museums. Several firings and paintings were involved to get the correct skintones on all parts of the body. Each doll comes with its own stand, and the stands were designed to fit together to make one display. *Courtesy Carmen Holshoe.*

Close-ups of the AFRIKA boy and girl show the exquisite facial details and the fine bead hand-work. *Courtesy Carmen Holshoe.*

Annette Himstedt's emphasis on realism shows in the number of glaze applications to achieve accurate skintones. Note doll construction and native costumes. *Courtesy Carmen Holshoe.*

26" LILL and 28" JILL are part of the 1992 Fantasy Children. They are also known as SCHWESTERN. JILL has salmon pink hair and eyes. LILL has green hair and eyes. These sisters reflect two different personalities. *Courtesy Himstedt advertisement.*

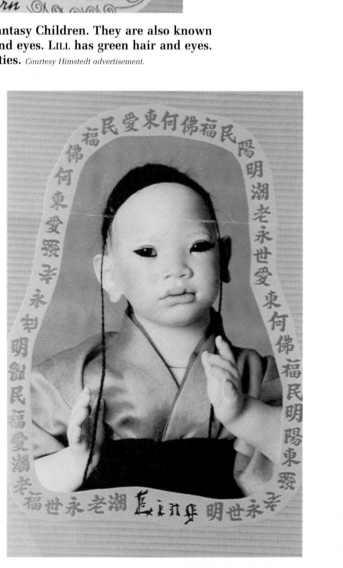

23" MING and LING are part of the 1992 Fantasy Children Series and are limited to 90 each. Both are exquisitely costumed in traditional Chinese dress. *Courtesy Himstedt advertisement.*

28" MOHINI is a girl from India and part of the Kinder Aus Porzellan Series of 1993. Limited to 80. MOHINI was nominated for Doll Award of Excellence in 1993. The facial and limb detail are just beautiful — including the jewel in her nose and forehead. Open mouth has great lip detail, and hands are outstanding. Workmanship on the clothes is perfect, especially the heavily beaded harem pants. *Courtesy Carmen Holshoe.*

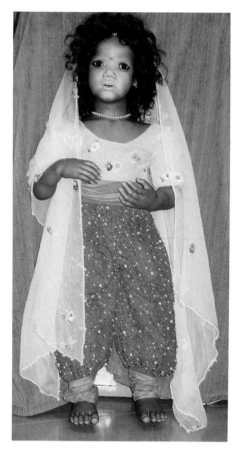

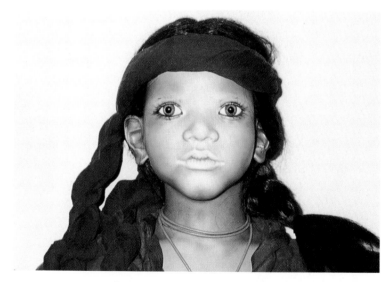

29" MOHAN is a boy from India and the brother of MOHINI. MOHAN'S outfit is made of silk, and he wears a silk braid around his forehead. He is a very detailed and wonderful doll. *Courtesy Carmen Holshoe.*

ARANA & DRAGAN represent a girl and boy from India and are part of the Kinder Aus Porzellan Series of 1993. Sizes are unknown. It has been reported that only 7 from an edition of 25 came to United States. *Courtesy Himstedt advertisement.*

26" ANNABELLA (left) and 28" ISA-BELITA (right) are part of the 1993 Kinder Aus Porzellan Series. *Courtesy Himstedt advertisement.*

23" NANJA (left) with red hair in braids and 28" MARIE-CLAIRE (right), also called GIRL WITH BOW, are from the 1993 Kinder Aus Porzellan Series. *Courtesy Himstedt advertisement.*

27" LATIE and 29" DALANAR are children from Tibet and from the 1994 Kinder Aus Porzellan Series. Limited to 80 each. *Courtesy Himstedt advertisement.*

29" SARITA and JONDAL are a girl and boy from India. They are part of the 1994 Kinder Aus Porzellan Series and limited to 70 each. *Courtesy Himstedt advertisement.*

26" MELA is an Irish girl with long red hair. She has green ruffled pants that extend beyond her dress to her shins. She is barefooted. MELA is a part of the Kinder Aus Porzellan Series and is limited to 90. *Courtesy Geri Cote.*

Two dolls from the 1994 Kinder Aus Porzellan Series. Left: 28" BLANDA, a girl of Griechenland, is limited to 80. Right: LUKA, a boy from Ireland, is limited to 90. *Courtesy Himstedt advertisement.*

AUSCHRA with red hair and FLORINDA with blonde hair are part of the 1994 porcelains and limited to 25 each. They sold out immediately at Toy Fair.
Courtesy Himstedt advertisement.

JOLANDE and JORINE are made of porcelain with cloth bodies. Both have a limited edition of 25 each. Both sold out at the February 1995 Toy Fair and are destined to be **very rare.** *Courtesy Annette Himstedt.*

Left is SHIANGI and right is MEI LI. Both are made of porcelain and cloth. 1995 dolls are limited to 80 each.
Courtesy Annette Himstedt.

From left to right are LINNE, LISBETH, and LASSE. All are made of porcelain with cloth bodies and limited to 90 each. *Courtesy Annette Himstedt.*

Left is KAJALI and right is MAYUKI from 1995 collection. Both are made of porcelain and cloth. Limited to 70 each.
Courtesy Annette Himstedt.

This photo was taken at the 1995 Toy Fair. From left to right: MAYUKI, KAJALI, Kathy Sneary who is the Annette Himstedt porcelain representative in the United States, and Gabriel from Germany who works with Annette Himstedt.

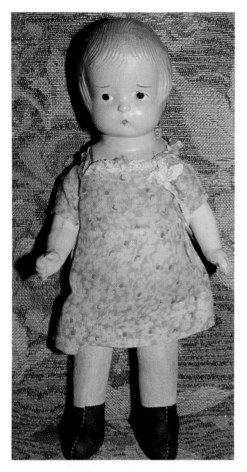

This 15" doll was made by the Chicago-based company of Rosie and Ira Hoffmann in the mid-1920s. They generally made all cloth children and boudoir (bed) dolls for the reasonably priced trade. This doll has no name but is shown in Hoffman's 1924 catalog at $7.66 a dozen. She was a pre-Patsy and was actually designed after the popular German doll called JUST ME which was made by Armand Marseille. $150.00. *Courtesy David Spurgeon.*

⁀ Horsman ⁀

Faced with the popularity of Madame Alexander's Cissy during the 1950s, Horsman decided to manufacture an upscaled line called "Couturier Division" with fashions from different designers. The doll, named Cindy, came in a 18–20" size in 1957.

By 1958, Horsman added a 10½" version of Cindy. She had sleep eyes with molded eyelashes, four slanted painted eyebrows, high heel feet, and a jointed waist. Her third and fourth fingers are molded together. Her quality is almost as good as other small fashion dolls, such as Little Miss Revlon, Little Miss Ginger, or the 10½" Toni. When found in mint condition, Cindy is a beautiful doll.

Horsman's Patsy look-a-likes, Sally and Dorothy, have their right arms bent at the elbow just like Patsy. The mold numbers of 160, 170, and 180 belong to Horsman.

In 1961, Horsman made Jacqueline which is marked "JK." She is a tall, thin lady doll with high heel feet. Her wardrobe consisted of very nicely designed and well made clothes. This same doll was sold as a blank (nude, undressed, and marked with another company name) for Kaysam.

It must be remembered there were only three companies who had the workers, factories, vats, materials, and costly upkeep to actually make dolls in the 1950s. There were other companies who made dolls as blanks for other companies to purchase, but as far as manufacturers/wholesalers, there was only Ideal, Horsman, and Effanbee.

Horsman came up with a composition formula in 1985 and has used it for special reissued dolls. All are of excellent quality, and the only difference between the old and new dolls is the newer material is shiny. Old composition is more muted. The following is the listing of these dolls: 1928 Baby (1985), Tynie Baby (1986), Hebee & Shebee (1987), Billikin and Ella Cinders (1988), Sister (1989), Baby Bright Eyes (1989), Dimples (1990), Brother and Dolly Record (1991), Buttercup (1992), and Baby Rosebud (1993).

18" ROSEBUD by Horsman is made of compositon with cloth body, tin sleep eyes, and mohair wig. All original with label pinned to front of dress. $300.00 up.
Courtesy Susan Girardot.

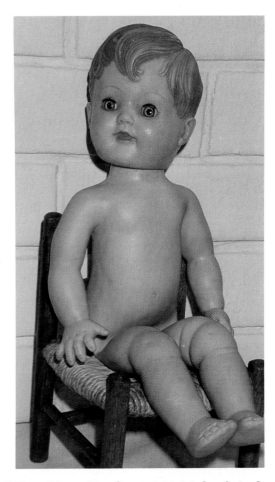

13" GOLD MEDAL BOY from 1955. Made of vinyl with one-piece body and limbs. Has excellent modeled head and marked "Horsman" on neck. $45.00. *Courtesy Pat Graff.*

Right: 18" RUTHIE from 1955. Also called FAIR SKIN DOLL. Made of early vinyl with rooted hair. Has one-piece stuffed body and limbs. (See molded hair version in *Modern Collector Dolls, Volume 3*, page 168.) $75.00. *Courtesy Kathy Tvrdik.*

17" all hard plastic CINDY with sleep eyes and dynal wig. Her name is CINDY STRUTTER if a walker. Made in 1956 and sold through catalog stores. Marked "170" on head. $200.00. *Courtesy Linda Shelton.*

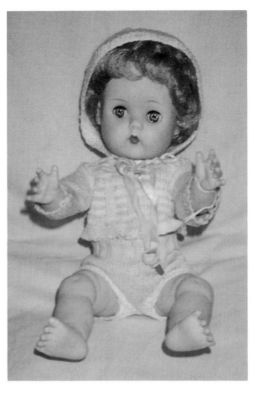

All vinyl BABY PRECIOUS is an excellent quality doll made from 1954 to 1956. Has dynel rooted hair and sleep eyes. Wearing some of her original clothes. $40.00. *Courtesy Linda Shelton.*

DRINKEE WALKER is made of vinyl and plastic with rooted hair and sleep eyes. Original, from 1988. $50.00. *Courtesy Linda Shelton.*

10½" CINDY dolls have jointed waists, sleep eyes, high heel feet, and original "undies." One on right has jointed knees. Made in 1958. Both are marked "Horsman" on the head. $75.00 each. *Courtesy Marie Ernst.*

This wonderful child's head was designed by Irene Szor for Horsman in 1973. It is a fashion head, and the hair can be styled in many ways. Also referred to as a makeup head. Since this one is jointed at the neck, it probably had a stand. $35.00. *Courtesy Linda Shelton.*

Horsman used the Irene Szor designed BETSY McCALL head as a hairstyle shoulderhead form for girls. Marked "Horsman/1971." $90.00. *Courtesy Linda Shelton.*

Left: 11" LITTLE DEBBIE advertsing doll made in 1972 by Horsman Doll Company. She was the 25th anniversary doll, and her head was designed by Irene Szor. Right: 11" porcelain and cloth LITTLE DEBBIE with glass eyes. Marked "Little Debbie 30th Anniversary" on head and "77" (1977). Both are original. Left - $35.00; right - $25.00. *Courtesy Kathy Tvrdik.*

1985 was the first year Horsman reissued one of their old dolls, and this one is a 1928 baby. The new composition is much like the old, only shinier. Has cloth body. Won the 1985 Doll of the Year Award. $165.00. *Courtesy Linda Shelton.*

Second in the series of earlier dolls made by Horsman. They are TYNE BABY TWINS, replicas of the older 1924 doll. $95.00 set. *Courtesy Linda Shelton.*

HEEBEE and SHEBEE were the third in the Horsman reissue series, sold in 1987. Both made of the new composition with painted features. Limited to 3,500 pieces each. The dolls were designed originally by Charles Twelvetrees. $150.00 set. *Courtesy Linda Shelton.*

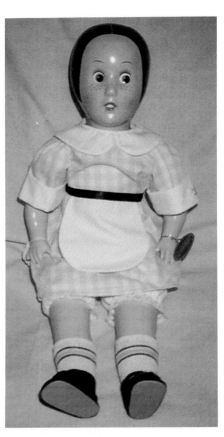

ELLA CINDER is one of the 1988 reproductions of old dolls by Horsman. Made of composition with painted features and molded hair. Original was on market in 1925. Limited to 3,000 pieces. $145.00. *Courtesy Linda Shelton.*

BILLIKEN is the other 1988 reproduction doll from the Horsman series. Has composition head with plush body and limbs. Originally made in 1909. Limited to 3,000. $78.00. *Courtesy Linda Shelton.*

Sixth in the series of reproduced dolls is SISTER who was originally on the market in 1937. Made of compostion with cloth body and painted eyes. Hair is molded to a peak. Made in 1989 and limited to 3,000. **$100.00.** *Courtesy Linda Shelton.*

Seventh in the reissue series is BRIGHT STAR baby made in 1989. Made of composition with cloth body. Limited to 2,000. **$155.00.** *Courtesy Linda Shelton.*

DIMPLES was chosen as the 125th anniversary doll and is the eighth to be reissued. Made of composition and cloth with a limited edition of 2,000. Made in 1990. **$175.00.** *Courtesy Linda Shelton.*

DOLLY ROSEBUD and BROTHER were the ninth in the series of Horsman reproductions. Made in 1991. **$200.00 each.** *Courtesy Linda Shelton.*

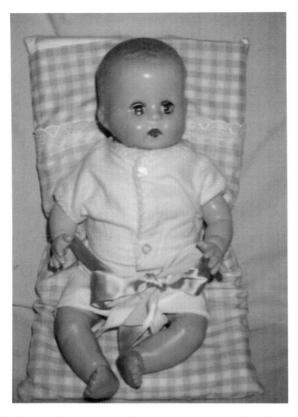

Tenth in the series is BUTTERCUP, a reproduction of the 1922 doll. Made in 1992 and limited to 2,000. **$90.00.** *Courtesy Linda Shelton.*

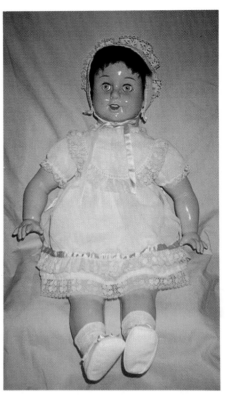

27" BABY ROSEBUD is eleventh in Horsman's special composition/cloth doll series. **$225.00.** *Courtesy Linda Shelton.*

Horsman's SOFTEE KIDS had softly stuffed body and limbs, vinyl mask face, and rooted hair on forehead. Made in 1991. **$15.00.** *Courtesy Linda Shelton.*

❧ Mary Hoyer ❧

Mary Hoyer owned a yarn shop in Reading, Pennsylvania, and sold a great deal of yarn and craft items through dime stores and mail order. She designed and produced pattern books for adult and children items. She came up with the idea to sell a doll with a pattern book for doll clothes. Since she was not in the doll business, Hoyer purchased blanks, mostly from the Frisch Doll Company, and designed patterns for the doll's wardrobe. A Hoyer doll will have a large circle incised in its back, and most have the name "Mary Hoyer" inside the circle. Some will also have "14"/made in USA" incised on the doll.

A very pretty dark haired MARY HOYER dressed in original crocheted outfit made from a Mary Hoyer pattern. $450.00. *Courtesy Jeannie Nespoli.*

14" all hard plastic MARY HOYER doll with sleep eyes. Dressed in original crocheted pattern outfit. $475.00.

Courtesy Jeannie Nespoli.

14" MARY HOYER doll with unusual red hair. Made of all composition with sleep eyes. Dressed in original sailor suit. $450.00 up. *Courtesy Jeannie Nespoli.*

Beautiful 14" factory dressed MARY HOYER doll. Made of all hard plastic with sleep eyes and mark. $500.00. *Courtesy Anita Pacey.*

14" all composition MARY HOYER doll with mohair wig and sleep eyes. Dressed in crocheted outfit made from original Mary Hoyer pattern. $450.00 up. *Courtesy Jeannie Mauldin.*

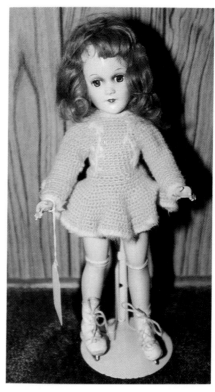

❧ Ideal ❧

Toni – a golden word to collectors – is worth a small fortune if found in mint condition, especially mint in the box. There is no doubt that Toni was one of the most played with dolls between Bye-Lo and Barbie. She had beautiful hair that could be curled "just like mommy's." Mothers were waving their own hair at home using the machineless method called Toni Home Permanent, and the beauty operators were wailing it would be the end of their business forever. There were even stories and rumors told that if an licenced operator was caught giving someone a home permanent that they could be fined and even go to jail.

During this time, the child was enjoying her doll and Toni Play Wave. The reason the hair could be waved/curled was it was made of Dupont nylon. It is interesting that each wig contained enough nylon to make seven pairs of 15 denier hose. The solutions used by the child were not harmful because they were made of water and sugar.

Toni was used for other dolls, but they had saran wigs. These dolls included Miss Curity and Mary Hartline, that also had extra makeup around their eyes.

In 1951, twelve Toni dolls, in various hair colors and with specially designed hairdos, were sent to Paris and dressed by the most famous designers of that day – Paquin, Gres, Carven, Heim, Lafaurie, Worth, Desses, Rouff, Paiquet, Patou, Bruyere, and Rochas. This was a collection kept by Ideal, and it was loaned out for display at various department stores. It would be interesting to know where the dolls in the collection are now.

The following is a listing of Toni sizes:

P-90 . . . . 14"
P-91 . . . . 16"
P-92 . . . . 19"
P-93 . . . . 21"
P-94 (rare) . . . . 22" – 23"

16" UNEEDA KID was an advertising doll made from 1914 to 1919 for Uneeda Biscuits. Made of composition with molded-on boots and cloth body. All original including box of biscuits (crackers). Looks very much like a Schoenhut wooden doll. In this mint condition - $600.00. *Courtesy Jeannie Mauldin.*

15" all composition BETTY JANE has glassene sleep eyes, dimpled chin, and exceptional detail to her fingers. Wearing original clothes. (If original clothes are tagged "Vogue," the doll is MARY JANE purchased from Ideal as a blank. Vogue dressed and marketed these dolls.) $375.00 up. *Courtesy June Schultz.*

16" BIT OF HEAVEN by Ideal Doll & Toys Co. Has mask face with painted features. The rest of the body is made of flannel plush, including the tops of wings (underneath side is felt). $70.00. *Courtesy Susan Girardot.*

22" P–94 MARY HARTLINE in extreme mint condition. Her arms are marked "P–93." (To see a different MARY HARTLINE, see the P–90 in green velvet and a V–91 with vinyl head in *Patricia Smith's Doll Values, Volume 8,* pg. 242.) $850.00 up. *Courtesy Susan Girardot.*

20" all composition MISS CURITY with glassene sleep eyes. Made by Ideal in 1949. All original. $465.00 up.

Courtesy Turn of Century Antiques.

This composition toddler is referred to as PLASSIE TODDLER. She was also shown in wholesale catalogs as SUZY TODDLER (1948) and BETSY TODDLER (1950–1953), a hard plastic version. Note the glassene eyes. Glassene was a by-product of World War II and can help date a doll. If this style toddler has tin or celluloid over tin sleep eyes, she would date from late 1920s to mid-1930s. After that date, eye materials became glass over metal, and the layers of glass would crack and craze. This doll is original. $265.00.

Courtesy Ellyn McCorkell.

18" vinyl MISS REVLON with rooted hair, sleep eyes, high heel feet, and swivel waist. Has beautiful face color. This doll has never been played with and is in mint condition. She also has her box. In this mint condition - $500.00 up.

Courtesy Cris Johnson.

17", 15", and 10½" MISS REVLON dolls. All are made of vinyl with swivel waists and high heel feet. All are original. 10½" - $95.00 up. 15" - $125.00 up each. 17" - $185.00 up. *Courtesy Sally Bethschieder.*

18" MISS REVLON with rare platinum rooted hair and dressed in rare outfit. This doll has never been played with and is in super mint condition. $500.00 up. *Courtesy Cris Johnson.*

10½" LITTLE MISS REVLON dressed in nightclothes. Mint condition - $95.00 up. *Courtesy Maureen Fukushima.*

10½" LITTLE MISS REVLON made of all vinyl with hard-to-find black rooted hair, jointed waist, and high heel feet. All original. $95.00 up. *Courtesy Maureen Fukushima.*

36" PATTI PLAYPAL dolls with varied hairstyles. Both have sleep eyes, and rooted hair. Both are all original and in mint condition. Each - $400.00 up. *Courtesy Edith Wise.*

36" PATTI PLAYPAL from 1959 and 38" PETER PLAYPAL from 1961. Both are all original and in mint condition. Each - $400.00 up. *Courtesy Edith Wise.*

26" vinyl and cloth PATTY PLAYPAL in her princess gown and tiara. She is a battery-operated talker whose eyes and face move when activated. She also has an aerobic outfit. Marked "Ideal Doll/1987." $165.00.

Two very beautiful 19" PATTI PETITE dolls (also called PETITE PLAYPAL). Both are original and in mint condition. They have their boxes. Mint condition - $700.00. Played with - $225.00. *Courtesy Cris Johnson.*

17" SCARECROW from the *Wizard of Oz* made by Ideal in 1939. Has cloth body and limbs with painted mask face and yarn hair. Looking at this doll, you can "see" Ray Bolger who played the part in the film. $800.00. *Courtesy Susan Girardot.*

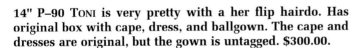

14" P–90 TONI is very pretty with a her flip hairdo. Has original box with cape, dress, and ballgown. The cape and dresses are original, but the gown is untagged. $300.00.

These two P–90 TONI dolls are dressed in very typical, original dresses. Each - $325.00.

14" P–90 TONI dressed in original jumper and blouse with replaced shoes. Made of hard plastic. $350.00.

Courtesy Mary Williams.

P–91 strung TONI with platinum nylon wig and wearing a very rare Toni dress with imbossed Scotty dogs. She is a 16" doll made of all hard plastic. $450.00 up.

Courtesy Susan Girardot.

16" TONI with beautiful white hair wearing tagged dress. Marked "P–92." Mint condition - $650.00. *Courtesy*

Elizabeth Montesano.

A very beautiful Toni in perfect, mint in box condition. Marked "P–93." $600.00. *Courtesy Mary Williams.*

These four dresses are all tagged and can all have variations of prints used. Each - $45.00 and up.

Ideal produced a doll inspired by "Velvet Brown," the character played by Lori Martin on the television show, *National Velvet*. This show was first telecast Sept. 18, 1960, and ran for two seasons. The program was based loosely on the English novel, *National Velvet,* which also had a 1944 movie version which starred Elizabeth Taylor. In the TV version, the setting was changed to a dairy farm in the American Midwest, and Velvet's throughbred

horse was named King. The stories revolved mainly around the girl and her horse, plus her family members and the farm's handyman.

In 1961, Ideal produced the Velvet Brown doll with an excellent likeness of the young actress. This doll came in 29", 32", 36", 38", and 42" sizes. At the same time, the company outfitted the body with multi-joints for a 25" and 29–30" doll and called her Miss Ideal at first, but decided to market her as Daddy's Girl.

(The period of 1960 to 1963 were the years of the *big girls* for all doll companies.) Daddy's Girl is Miss Ideal, and the smaller versions were taken from the 42" size. To confuse the issue a little more, Ideal wanted to use the body parts on another doll in 1962 and marketed Miss Ideal as Terry Twist. Ideal sold the body molds to American Character in October 1962, and they proceeded to make their multi-jointed Betsy McCall. Later, the bodies were sold to the Empire-Crossman Plastics Moulds Co. Inc. and they apparently sold abroad.

There is one common demoninator for the 42" dolls – they all have long, below the shoulder hair that is slightly wavy and cut straight across. Miss Ideal and Terry Twist have waist length hair with one version as a beautiful platium blonde. There are exceptions – Miss Ideal can have heavy below the shoulder hair with heavy full bangs and Terry Twist can have curly, wavy, just to the shoulders hair with a side part.

The above information is courtesy of the public library and these men who were involved with toy research and development – James Goldberg, Lonny Houseman, and Ira Goinhorst.

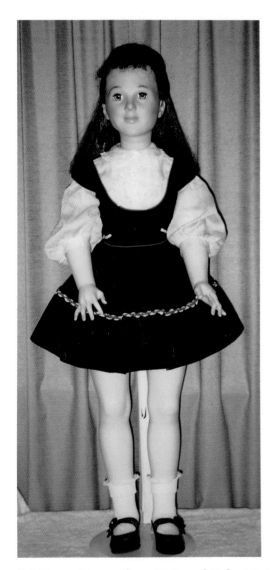
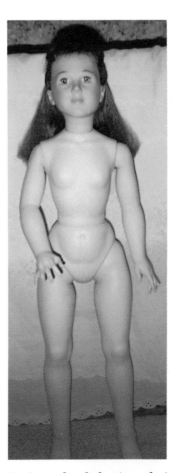
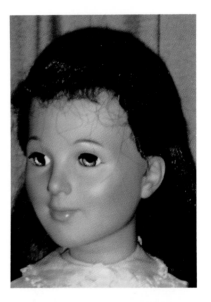
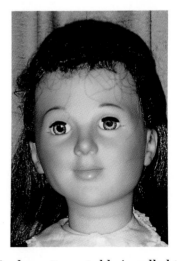

42" Velvet Brown from *National Velvet* TV series is made of plastic and vinyl. Has brunette rooted hair pulled to top and fastened in back. She is extremely well modeled and very posable with multiple joints. Her original one-piece jumper outfit has an organdy bodice, attached half slip with red satin lining, and trimmed skirt. There was a leg seam at the crotch, and to dress, the doll had to "step" into the outfit. Marked on head "Metro Goldwyn Mayer Inc. (owners of the copyright)/MFG. by Ideal Toy Corp." and on back "Ideal Toy Co./G-42". $875.00. *Courtesy Edith Wise.*

42" VELVET shown with a smaller version that is also all original. 42" - $875.00; smaller version - $500.00.
Courtesy Edith Wise.

Smaller version of VELVET dressed in short-sleeved plaid blouse, jeans, and detailed boots. All original. $500.00. *Courtesy Edith Wise.*

Close-up of VELVET BROWN doll. *Courtesy Edith Wise.*

18" ANNE OF GREEN GABLES (WAITING AT THE STATION) was made by Irwin of Canada in 1994. She is vinyl with cloth body, inset green eyes, and red rooted hair. Also made in 1993 in porcelain in several different costumes. $40.00. *Courtesy Pat Graff.*

11½" THE FATHER-TO-BE made of plastic and vinyl with bendable knees and painted wedding band. Marked "Judith" on back. Paper tag marked "Made in Japan." White couple has smiling expressions. African American expectant parents have serious expressions. (See African American MOTHER-TO-BE in *Patricia Smith's Doll Values, Tenth Series*, page 251). $30.00.

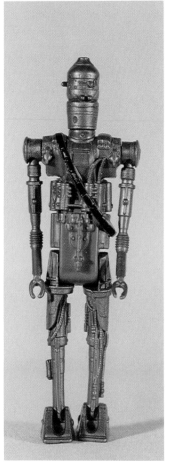

Left: 13" IG-88 is a character from the movie, *Star Wars*, and was made in 1978. Marked "G.M.F.G.I." for General Mills Food Group, Inc. This is one of the most elusive figures from the early *Star Wars* large figure set. Why Kenner bothered to make this figure is unknown. This robot had such a small role in the movie, he is hard to detect. $375.00.

Center and right: 8½" JAWA is also from the movie, *Star Wars*, and he is marked "Kenner." Center photo shows him with a hooded cloth coat over his molded vinyl hood. The photo on the right shows him with the cloth hood removed. (Variation of this figure can be seen in *Patricia Smith's Doll Values, Series 10*, page 253.) $65.00.

19" CHOCOLATE STRAWBERRY SHORTCAKE BABY is made of vinyl with cloth body, red rooted hair, painted features, and freckles. Has sweet scent. Original and marked "American Greeting/Corp./1982/ Made in Hong Kong." $40.00.

Action figures based on the movie and TV cartoon series, *Ghostbusters*. Both 1988 sets came with ghost. Left: EGON SPENGLER's jaw drops open and his neck extends. His tie also pops up. Right: WINSTON ZEDDMORE's head rotates 360° and his mouth opens. Each, with accessories - $35.00–40.00. (See variations in *Modern Collector Dolls, Volume 7*, pg. 174.)

JANINE from *Ghostbusters* playset made by Kenner in 1988. Her glasses and eyes bug out. Also her jaw drops and forelock flips up. Shown with ghost fighting accessory and ghost. $30.00.

19" CLAUDIA KISHI of THE BABYSITTERS CLUB. She is an Oriental doll with fixed earrings and angled cut bangs. Made in 1993. $48.00. *Courtesy LeeAnn Geary.*

Close-up of CLAUDIA KISHI and STACEY MCGILL, part of THE BABYSITTERS CLUB collection made by Kenner. Each - $48.00. *Courtesy LeeAnn Geary.*

Kerr & Hinz

Bisque dolls that have a resemblance to Nancy Ann Storybook dolls, but marked K & H, were made by Kerr & Hinz of Santa Clara, Cailfornia. The company was actually the Santa Clara Tile Company with a building that was condemned in 1968, but not torn down until 1973. The painted bisque dolls were found stored in the deserted building and sold to collectors. From information found, many of the nude dolls were sold to church groups to be dressed and then resold at festivals. One order, dated 1947, was for 1,000 dolls.

The basic 7" girl doll, named Peg O' My Heart, is jointed at the shoulders only. She came in a box with blue or pink dots. The 4" baby is jointed at the shoulders and hips and has bent baby legs. Arms on the boy and girl dolls are very thin.

From company records, 7" undressed dolls wholesaled for $7.20 a dozen while 7" dressed dolls sold $7.50 a dozen. It's interesting that the price difference is so close between the nude and dressed dolls. The 4" babies sold for $3.80 per dozen.

7" PEG O' MY HEART doll named MISS AUBURN from 1947. Made of bisque and jointed at shoulders only. Marked "K&H/USA." $95.00. *Courtesy Glorya Woods.*

7" BRIDEMAID using the PEG O' MY HEART bisque doll of 1947. Marked "K&H/USA." $95.00. *Courtesy Glorya Woods.*

5½" bisque RINGBEARER for the wedding party. Made of bisque and jointed at shoulders only. Marked "K&H." $125.00. *Courtesy Glorya Woods.*

7" PRINCE CHARMING (left) and DUTCH BOY (right) are made of bisque with jointed shoulders only. The clothes are sewn onto the dolls. Prince - $145.00. Dutch - $125.00. *Courtesy Glorya Woods.*

These original dolls were made by Kathe Kruse in 1984. All are made of vinyl and cloth with stitched fingers. Left to right: BINE, ANSELM, and NICOLAS. Each - $425.00–475.00. *Courtesy Pat Graff.*

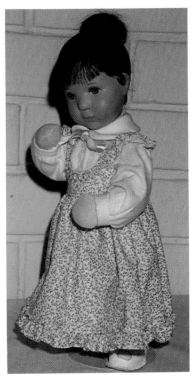

14" NICOLA is made of vinyl and cloth with stitched fingers. Made by Kathe Kruse in 1993 and limited to 50. Original - $400.00. *Courtesy Pat Graff.*

10" KATHKLIN (right) from 1984 and 10" GUSTI (left) from 1991 were made by Kathe Kruse. Both originals are made of vinyl and cloth with painted features and human hair wigs. They are also posable. Each - $280.00–285.00. *Courtesy Pat Graff.*

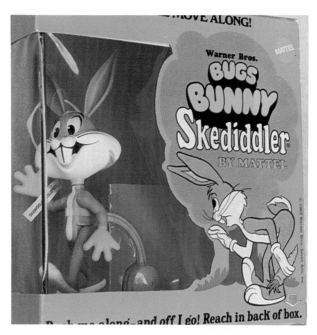

Wonderful BUGS BUNNY SKEDIDDLER has wheels, and when pushed, the legs move in walking motion. Made by Mattel in 1966. Mint in box - $85.00. *Courtesy Cris Johnson.*

BABY LOVE LIGHT has vinyl head and hands with one-piece cloth body and limbs. Hands are cupped for holding hands with child. Battery-operated eyes light up when hands are pressed. After child goes to sleep and the hands fall away, the light goes out. Marked "1970 Mattel Inc./Mexico" on head, but was marketed in 1971. $25.00. *Courtesy David Spurgeon.*

16" BABY SKATES made by Mattel in 1983. She is a wind-up skater made of rigid vinyl with painted features. $40.00. *Courtesy Kathy Tvrdik.*

14" LIL' BIT COUNTRY dolls have vinyl heads and limbs, cloth bodies, rooted hair, and sleep eyes. Made by Mattel in 1992. Both are original. Each - $25.00. *Courtesy Pat Graff.*

18" WHERE'S WALDO shown with his friend, WENDA. Both have vinyl heads with gauntlet hands and feet. Cloth bodies and limbs have wires for posing. Clothes make their bodies, and caps are glued onto molded hair. Their belts have a printed WALDO scene with magnifying glass "Find Waldo" buckles. Both are marked "MHI 1990" on neck and tagged "Mattel, Inc./El Segundo, Ca. 90245 U.S.A./Made in China/Where's Waldo?™/Martin Handford 1991." His trusty dog, WOOF, is 9½" tall with plastic glasses sewn to head. Plush and sewn-on clothes make his body. His magnifying glass collar is missing. Each - $28.00. *Courtesy LeeAnn Geary.*

19" HOT LOOKS doll, MIMI, represents France. She has a vinyl head with rooted hair and painted features. Stockinette body has sewn-on bra and panties. Also has vinyl gauntlet hands and wire armiture for posing. All original. Marked "Mattel, Inc. 1986." Others dolls in the HOT LOOKS set are STACEY, the American girl with black hair and brown eyes; ELKIE from Sweden dressed in exercise clothes; CHELSEA, the London adventurer; ZIZI, the African dancer with black hair and brown eyes. Each - $55.00. *Courtesy Pat Graff.*

⤙ Mdvanii ⤚

Mdvanii was first introduced in 1989 by Billyboy™ of Paris, a reknown designer of jewelry and clothes collections. Soon, she was news around the world. Each doll is entirely handmade and anatomically correct. Each Mdvanii doll has a metal tag on back of her neck to ensure authenticity. Alexandre of Paris designs her fabulous hairstyles, and her designer clothes reflect Parisan high fashions, truly the finest created for any 11½" doll.

1990 Mdvanii styles were photographed by famous photographer, Antoine Giacomoni. The first market (retail) prices on these dolls ranged from $165.00 to $850.00. The secondary market prices (current values) are: boudoir or street clothes - $500.00 up; ballgowns - $1,200.00–1,900.00. Gift sets start at $1,600.00. *Photos courtesy BillyBoy™.*

12½" DECKER is the most difficult figure to find from the Mego collection based on *Star Trek, The Motion Picture.* Marked "PPC" on head and "Mego Corp. 1975/Made in Hong Kong" on lower back. $265.00.

Courtesy Phyllis Kates.

8" PLANET OF THE APES action figures. Marked "APJAC Prdo. Inc. Twenth Century Fox Films. 1974." Body-marked "Mego. Reg. U.S. Pat. office. Made in Hong Kong. 1971." Each - $22.00. *Courtesy Kathy Tvrdik.*

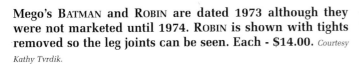

Mego's BATMAN and ROBIN are dated 1973 although they were not marketed until 1974. ROBIN is shown with tights removed so the leg joints can be seen. Each - $14.00. *Courtesy Kathy Tvrdik.*

12½" Sᴏɴɴʏ & Cʜᴇʀ dolls made of all vinyl with extra joints. Cʜᴇʀ's body was used for several other dolls. Both marked "Mego 1975." Each - $20.00. *Courtesy David Spurgeon.*

There were many outfits available for the Cʜᴇʀ doll. She is shown here in the American Indian costume from 1975. $25.00.

11½" Lᴀᴠᴇʀɴᴇ ᴀɴᴅ Sʜɪʀʟᴇʏ from the TV show by the same name. ("Laverne" was played by Penny Marshall and "Shirley" by Cindy Williams.) Made by Mego in 1977, and both dolls are original. (These dolls have been shown in another volume of this series, but not in color or in this mint condition.) Each - $25.00. *Courtesy Margaret Mandel.*

⤳ Richard Metzler ⤳

The wonderful marionettes in this section were fashioned from the hands of the master carver, Richard Metzler II, who made them for Richard Oberender (1858–1919). They were made to entertain children and adults who attended the 1893 Exposition held in Amsterdam. After the exposition, the set was put on display at the Oberender factory, along with a bronze medal won by the company that year. It must be noted that Richard Metzler was also a noted illustrator, so if the figures "look familiar," you may have seen them in old children's books. This set is courtesy Diane French and The Grand Lady Museum at Chance Pond in West Franklin, NH. The value of each figure is unknown, although experts in Europe have made offers for all eight figures.

10" MOTHER

10" RED RIDING HOOD

10" GRANDMOTHER

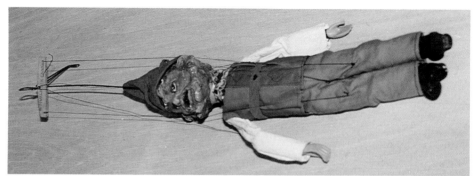

12" WOODSMAN

10" BOY

11½–12" WOLF

20½" DONKEY with curled mohair tail

10" WITCH

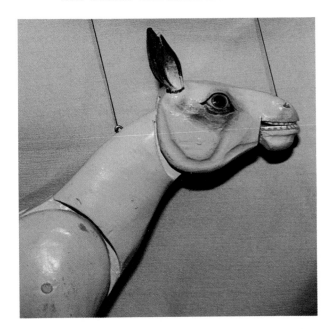

Mollye

Mollye Goldman of Molly-es International, Molly-es Doll Outfitter, and Hollywood Cinema Fashions was a very good friend of mine from the early 1970s to her death. For information about her and her company, I refer you to *Modern Collector Dolls, Volume 3,* pages 71–88 in the Doll Artist section. Actual factory photographs are included in the Eegee section of *Modern Collector Dolls, Volume 5,* page 100–102, and again from page 232–241. Also *Modern Collector Dolls, Volume 4,* pages 184–219, includes photos of Mollye herself.

I would like to say a few things about Mollye, the woman. She was a bubbly lady, barely five-foot tall, who loved to hum, sing, and talk. Her husband, Meyer, used to tell me he would sometimes pretend to listen to her and got by with it because he nodded his head from time to time. (A common practice of husbands in many households!) Mollye loved people, especially children, to the point she would rather be out among them – at a shop, the market, the zoo, or a museum. Her favorite times were sitting on a bench, engaging in conversations with whoever joined her. Mollye cared about other people, and she had the ability to find out all about their lives.

This is not the description of a hardcore, very needful, competitive businesswoman at all, especially in the 1930s and 1940s. Mollye was the world's biggest "patsy" – the believer in every dream and every person's word. If she had been more aggressive, she certainly would have been the most remarkable dollmaker of her era. Had it not been for her husband, Meyer, and a fantastic business manager, she might not have had a business.

Let us go on to a few important items. My grandmother often said there are three sides to any story – theirs, yours, and the truth. All I know is Mollye's side of this story concerning Johnny Gruelle, the author of the Raggedy Ann series. The Goldmans became good friends with Johnny Gruelle and visited his Florida home. According to Mollye, there was an understanding between the two of them that Mollye would make the Raggedy dolls, each with her signature in ink on their chest. Johnny asked her to patent her face designs because he felt they actually looked better than the older ones. Based on a "handshake" agreement, Mollye was to design the faces, make the dolls, and be paid a percentage because of their friendship. It was a workable arrangement until the unforseen happened – Johnny Gruelle died.

Myrtle Gruelle, Johnny's widow, asked Mollye to stop making the Raggedys. At first, Mollye refused because Johnny Gruelle's patent #107,328 of 1915 had expired and had not been renewed. She had patents on the new items, #363,008 and #363,226. Also, Mollye continued making the dolls while the Gruelle family formed their own company, which took time and effort since the original patent holder was deceased.

Mollye gave her patents over to Myrtle Gruelle of her own freewill. Mrs. Gruelle, within the terms of a pre-arranged agreement, immediately sold the rights to the dolls to the Knickerbocker Toy Company.

It has been rumored that Mollye Goldman made over $1 million in two years, (1936–1938) on the Raggedys alone! If true, Mollye Goldman dolls would be everywhere, *just everywhere.* Her dolls are as hard, sometimes harder, to find then the elusive Volland's versions. Few people could afford the $3.89 for a Mollye's doll – a whopping amount for any doll during the Depression. Those years were not good times for anyone to make $1 million.

Consider one more item for "the other side of the story." It has been "reported" that the United States Supreme Court ruled in favor of Myrtle Gruelle. When I asked Mollye about this, she just giggled in a child-like manner. "Now Patricia," she answered, "why would those fine gentlemen in Washington, D.C.

want to be bothered with the likes of a case like that...even if there were one?" Mollye wasn't Irish but sometimes pretend to be, especially when wanting to express a point. If anyone doubts Mollye's story, please see *Plaything Magazine* advertisement on page 198 of *Modern Collector Dolls, Volume 4.*

Does it really matter? The only thing that really matters is Mollye Goldman was keeping her word to Johnny Gruelle. When asked, she stopped Raggedy doll production rather than file a lawsuit, since she was the one who held the lawful patents.

For any collector who is fortunate enough to have a Mollye Goldman Raggedy Ann, Raggedy Andy, or Beloved Belindy, *treasure it!* It is a part of American history. Also remember why the dolls were made in the first place. Johnny Gruelle, out of love for his dying little girl, Marcella, created his Raggedy Ann and Andy stories to amuse his child and ease her pain.

Extremely rare all cloth BELOVED BELINDY made by Mollye Doll Outfitters. This photograph is a company original used in advertisements. If this doll was on the market, it would have been in a very limited quanity. $1,400.00 up.

Entire grouping of composition dolls based on the movie, *Thief of Bagdad*. They were made by Hollywood Cinema Fashions, a Mollye Goldman company. On the backdrop is an illustration of SABU, the Indian boy from the movie, and there is also a doll of him. All are considered very rare, especially the male figures. $500.00–1,000.00. *Photo by Mollye Studios.*

20" all hard plastic BRIDE made by Molly-es' Hollywood Cinema Fashions. This doll is unmarked but was made 1952–1954. (It must be remembered, like several other companies, Mollye Goldman purchased blank, unmarked dolls to dress and market.) This is same doll used for NANCY ANN STYLESHOW dolls. $485.00. *Courtesy Jeannie Nespoli.*

16" cloth INTERNATIONAL DOLL made by Mollye. Her logo label can be seen on the apron. She has a mask face with oil-painted features and black yarn hair. $125.00.

21" ROSETTE is an unmarked doll dressed by Mollye Goldman in 1955 as part of the Evening in Paris perfume display at Philadelphia's Wanamaker's Store. She is made of all hard plastic with sleep eyes and saran wig. She was also sold to the general public for $19.99. $450.00. *Courtesy Jeannie Nespoli.*

CHRIS, THE AMERICAN AIRLINES STEWARDESS was made by Mollye in mid-1950s. Made of all hard plastic and came in 14", 18", 23", 28" sizes. Could also be purchased with case filled with accessories. Original except for shoes and missing hose. 14" -$225.00; 18" - $325.00; 23" - $425.00; 28" - $700.00. *Courtesy Bonnie Stewart.*

18" all hard plastic BETTY ELIZABETH with sleep eyes and original gown. Roses in hair added. Originally had gardenia coronet hairpiece. When asked why she gave dolls a name and a nickname together, Mollye replied, "I love double names! I often put myself to sleep making up names for twin boys and girls." Made in 1954. $445.00. *Courtesy Sharon McDowell.*

Harold Naber

It is not possible to say enough about this artist; too little would sound philosophical, so I will try for a happy medium. To understand an artist's work, especially woodcarvers, one must know a little about that person. The same applies to the art of dollmaking. If a doll is pleasing and its workmanship superb, the owner will want to know more about the doll's creator to fully appreciate their doll's beauty and uniqueness.

Harold P. Naber is as man of dedication to a dream. He is a man who has pursued that dream in several forms, including his Naber Kids and Wildwood Babies. All have a purpose which evolved from his dream. That dream continues to evolve with each new thought and idea that enhances his desire for perfection within conflict – a conquering of the world in his own manner.

That chosen manner is through his "Kids" and "Babies." They vary from the very young to the very old; from the happy to the sad. They come from all walks of life and are carved from all colors of woods found throughout the world. Yet, they all have one common demoninator, one thing to makes them the same – they all have green painted eyes. This symbolism is true to Naber's heart and represents a smile of tolerance. The green eyes mean that no matter how different someone is on the outside (or the number of rings on their trees), we are all a part of this planet we call our world.

According to Harold Naber, the near future is wide open for an animated TV series about the Kids and Babies. It will show them living their lives, having fun, and solving all their world's mysteries together.

These WILD WOOD BABIES are enjoying a perfect day in the sun. Left to right: CLARENCE, GISELA, and JOE. Each - $220.00. *Courtesy Naber Gestalt Company.*

1,001 is the magic number! That is the production number for all the Naber Babies. The following is a listing of who is available:

Name	Description	Introduced
Bernhard	Railroad Engineer	3/29/94
Horace	Cross-eyed child	4/1/94
Elizabeth	Little girl w/blanket	4/7/94
Bernice	Little bib dress	4/10/94
Van	Eskimo outfit	4/13/94
Natasha	Eskimo outfit	4/15/94
Kilo	Sleeping Eskimo baby	5/1/94
Michael	Business suit	7/30/94
Duffy	Baseball outfit	8/5/94
Vern	Golfer	8/8/94
Wanda	Playdress	9/8/94
Claudine/Claude	Twins	9/9/94
Tina (Sassafras wood)	Pinafore dress	9/13/94
Tina (Ebony walnut)	Fancy hair	9/13/94
Rufus	Sailor outfit	9/30/94
Martin	Farmer w/floppy hat	11/30/94
Martin (Ebony walnut)		11/30/94
Jolli (Golden or Ebony)	Rodeo Clown	12/8/94
Jan	Dutch boy w/wood shoes	12/16/94
Erika	Dutch girl w/wood shoes	12/16/94
Carol	Sailor girl	1/6/95
Emma	Top knot	2/1/95
Polli	Cowgirl	2/1/95
Alma	Watermelon dress	5/10/95
Mystik	Indian boy	5/3/95
Forget Me Not	Indian girl	5/3/95
Wolfgang	Bavarian boy	5/8/95
Gretchen	Bavarian girl	5/8/95
Melven	Baby cook	5/14/95
Theresa	Romper	5/21/95
Loui	Artist outfit	7/18/95
Tobi	Fireman w/carved helmet	7/20/95

CLUB AND CONVENTION BABIES

Name	Date	Issue (Sold Out)
Alexander	3/25/94	200
Eileen	4/30/94	200
Angel	4/1/95	300
Bill w/molded helmet	4/30/95	193

From the regular line, Elizabeth is sold out, and the following are getting very close to a sell out (most likely they will be by this book publication): Ivan, Natasha, and Bernice.

BIG WALLIE made in 1971. One sold in 1990 for $600.00. No other price known. *Courtesy Harold Naber.*

Left: LITTLE NUNI from 1972. $485.00. Center: TAMI from 1973. Value unknown. Right: SOURDOUGH from 1974. Anyone owning this figure is fortunate indeed. Value unknown. *Courtesy Harold Naber.*

Left: CHEECHAKO from 1974. Value in 1991 was $350.00. Right: TIPPER from 1975. Price unknown.
Courtesy Harold Naber.

Alaska Life Collection by Harold Naber in 1980. Left to right: CHIEF - $900.00; BIG SISTER - $375.00 up; LITTLE BROTHER - $300.00. *Courtesy Harold Naber.*

Harold Naber carvings from 1981. Left to right: SLEEPY JOE - $275.00 up; LITTLE TOM - $225.00; SILLY BILLY - $250.00.
Courtesy Harold Naber.

Left: MINI MO from 1981. $225.00. Right: LONA LISA from 1982. $175.00. *Courtesy Harold Naber.*

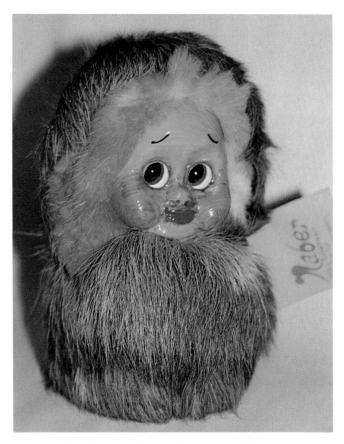

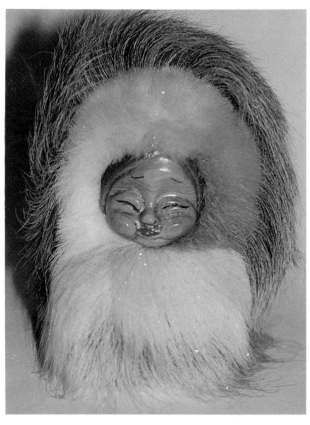

BIG TUNDRA TONYA from 1981. $200.00.

Courtesy Harold Naber.

TINY TUNDRA TONYA from 1981. $225.00.

Courtesy Harold Naber.

14" MILLI MOLLI was the first doll made by Naber Doll Company in 1979. Original face was carved from yellow cedar. Has cloth body. $1,000.00 up. *Courtesy Cecilia White.*

17" SALLY (left) and GEORGE (right) were carved in 1984 and command a very high price on the secondary market. Each - $1,050.00. *Courtesy Cecilia White.*

Left and far right is JAKE with MAX in the middle. ASHLEY is sitting down in front. They were the second, third, and fourth Naber Kids. (MOLLI was the first.) JAKE - $1,300.00; MAX - $1,100.00; ASHLEY - $775.00. *Courtesy Cecilia White.*

In the opinion of Harold Naber (this author, too!), BABY KILO, the sleeping Eskimo baby, is one of the cutest dolls made by the company. $165.00.

Courtesy Linda Shelton.

10" LITTLE ROSIE and IGOR were made in 1985. Although the letter from Naber Gestalt Co. stated that their hands and mukluks were made of solid casted high density urethane, this LITTLE ROSIE has cloth hands and mukluks. Both are on special woodgrained display stands that are imprinted "Naber." LITTLE ROSIE wears a Nunivak Island style parka. IGOR wears a St. Lawrence Island style parka. LITTLE ROSIE - $850.00; IGOR - $875.00 up.

Courtesy Cecilia White.

12" ALASKA BABIES with vinyl heads and arms. The eyes are closed. Very unusual and rare. Limited to 400. Each - $185.00 up. *Courtesy Cecilia White.*

These are all NABER KIDS and WILD WOOD BABIES. Top row: SISSI (with hurt foot?), MISHI, HOEY, AMY BABY, and AMY GIRL. Middle row: SISSI, WALTER, FRIEDA, PETER, and MAXINE. Bottom row: JAN, ERICA, and CAROL. All are original and all belong to owner Judith Smith. $400.00 to $650.00.

Upper left: MARTIN, the farmer with a large floppy hat. Introduced 11/30/94. $135.00.

Upper right: JOLLI, the rodeo clown. He has earned great respect by diverting bulls away from downed cowboys. Introduced 12/8/94. $145.00.

Lower right: A very thoughtful MYSTIK, an Indian boy whose introduction date was 5/3/95. All 1,001 pieces will soon be sold out. $130.00 up.

5½" ONE, TWO BUTTON MY SHOE is a bisque Nancy Ann Storybook doll with painted-on, side-buttoned boots. She is jointed at the shoulders only. Original. $145.00 and up. *Courtesy Glorya Woods.*

5½" NELLIE BIRD, NELLIE BIRD is a bisque Nancy Ann Storybook doll with box and wrist tag. $145.00 up. *Courtesy Pat Graff.*

4½" #85 FLOWERGIRL is a Nancy Ann Storybook doll made of all bisque. All original and in mint condition. $125.00. *Courtesy Shirley Doll Shop.*

5" NANCY ANN STORYBOOK DOLL is made of all hard plastic and has sleep eyes. Jointed at neck, shoulders, and hips. All original. $55.00 and up. *Courtesy Kathy Tvrdik.*

MUFFIE ICE SKATER, #903-1953, is a strung doll with no eyebrows. Marked "Storybook Dolls/Calif." **$225.00 up.** *Courtesy Maureen Fukushima.*

7½" all hard plastic MUFFIE walker, style #208/400, with saran wig. All original with box. **$245.00 up.** *Courtesy Elizabeth Montesand.*

A booklette came with MUFFIE dolls to show all the outfits that were available for her in 1954.
Each outfit - $175.00 up.

A booklette came with MUFFIE to show all the outfits that were available for her in 1954.
Each outfit - $175.00 up.

Each of these 10½" MISS NANCY ANN dolls are made of all vinyl and have rooted hair, sleep eyes, and swivel waist. They are all original and marked on the head. Each - $140.00 up. *Courtesy Marie Ernst.*

A wooden Nancy Ann Storybook display case with original finish. There were also hanging wall cases. $300.00 up. *Courtesy Sandy Johnson Barts.*

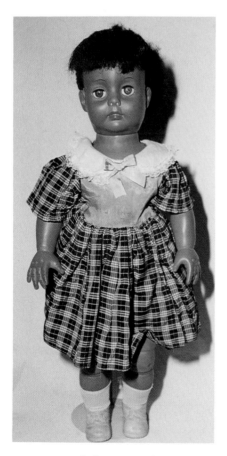

20" BLUETTE was made by Natural in 1955. Has vinyl head, sleep eyes, rooted hair, and stuffed one-piece vinyl body with limbs. Wearing original dress with replaced shoes and socks. $35.00. *Courtesy Kathy Tvrdik.*

36" WALKING BESS made by Natural Doll Co. in 1961. This is a very well made doll. Marked "AE5651/55" on head. (Dolls marked "AE 3651" are white dolls.) "Walking" means if the arm is held, the legs can be moved easily. $350.00. *Courtesy Phyllis Kates.*

⌦ Mel Odom ⌫

Mel Odom is a well-known illustrator and an extremely nice person. In the past 20 years, Odom has had his work exhibited at many great museums as well as the Society of Illustrators where he has twice received their Award of Excellence. Much can be said about this designer, but let's focus our attention to his doll creation, Gene.

Mel Odom wanted to create a doll that represented the "old" Hollywood – where a star blazed through the skies of Beverly Hills to encircle the world. He wanted his doll to represent the "dream" of every pretty girl in America, which was to see their name in lights, be on the big screen, and ultimately win the Academy Award, the "Oscar" which said it all – they had made it!

Gene was "discovered" when she worked as an usherette, and she is available in this costume with her accessories, a flashlight and hat. Gene watched the big screen and had played the parts along with her favorite actresses so many times that she could play their parts in her dreams. Soon she was making dreams for other girls waiting to be discovered. Discover her yourself. Order a brochure from Ashton-Drake Galleries, 9200 North Maryland Ave., Niles, IL 60714-9853.

15" GENE **was sculpted by Mel Odom and made by Ashton-Drake Galleries. She is made of all vinyl with extremely good quality. She is reasonably priced for a child to play with, yet has the fine craftsmanship and excellent wardrobe that collectors desire. $69.95.** *Courtesy Mel Odom.*

Left: "Striking Gold" is what GENE wore when she received the Golden Star Award. The resounding applause was not only for GENE's acting talents but for her beauty and the graceful acceptance speech. Center: Hollywood stars were asked to cheer the boys in the war, and many became almost as famous for being pin-up girls. GENE was one of those girls. This outfit is called"Crimson Sun." Right: 15" GENE dressed in her usherette outfit. She was working at the theater the night she was "discovered." This is a wonderfully designed outfit. All outfits can be ordered separately from Ashton-Drake for only $35.00. Doll - $69.95. *Courtesy Mel Odom.*

15" AMANDA was put on the market by Olmec in 1990. She is made of vinyl with cloth body, sleep eyes, and rooted hair. All original. $20.00. *Courtesy Pat Graff.*

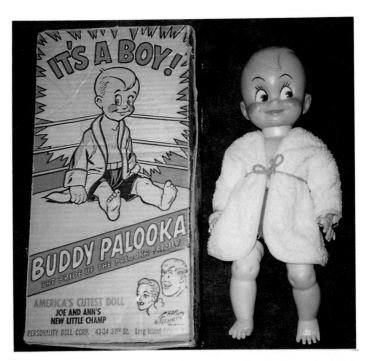

16" BUDDY PALOOKA was made by Personality Doll Co. in 1953. He is the son of comic strip characters, Joe and Ann Palooka. Has soft vinyl one-piece stuffed body, molded hair, and oversized painted eyes. All original with box. Mint in box - $600.00; played with nude doll - $200.00. *Courtesy Chris McWilliams.*

14" "Cherise" was made by Olmec in 1989. She is all vinyl with oversized sleep eyes and rooted hair. All original. $14.00. *Courtesy Pat Graff.*

4" SATURNIA of the CELESTRA QUEEN transforming dolls made by Placo Toys. Backpack is wings that snap off. Marked "Hong Kong" on lower back. $8.00. *Courtesy Kathy Tvrdik.*

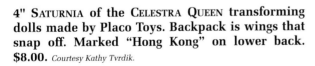

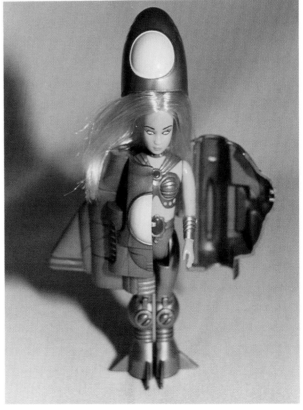

Pleasant Company

The American Girl Collection by the Pleasant Company is a great doll concept. It was created by the company's founder, Pleasant T. Rowland, noted educator and author of children's reading and language arts books used by schools.

There are five dolls in the series (blanks made by Gotz of Germany) — Felicity, a colonist from 1771; Kristen, an immigrant from 1854; Addy, a freed slave child from 1864; Samantha, a Victorian girl from 1904; and Molly, a girl facing World War II from 1944. Each doll has a series of five books telling about special events in their lives. Their storybooks are available in bookstores or from the Pleasant Company.

Each doll is factory dressed in a certain time period outfit. Accessories that accent the era are also included. Additional outfits and accessories — all historically accurate — can be purchased separately for the dolls. Items such as a wardrobe trunk, furniture, hobby or sewing articles, a music box, and their own doll can be added to the doll's collection.

What continues to be a unique feature of this company is its catalog. The public can only purchase the dolls and their accessories through the catalog. (The only items that can be purchased outside the Pleasant Company are book-related items and their magazine, *American Girl*.) To order a catalog, contact: The Pleasant Doll Company, P.O. Box 620190, Middleton, WI. 53562-0190 or telephone 1-800-845-0005.

It must be noted that other companies have started producing doll series similar to The American Girl Collection, but remember, *the original is usually the best.*

18" SAMANTHA PARKINGTON from THE AMERICAN GIRL COLLECTION is dressed in sailor's outfit that was purchased separately. It includes a bo'sn's whistle on neckcord. She is made of vinyl with cloth body. Has rooted hair, sleep eyes with lashes, and open/closed mouth with two teeth. Marked on neck "©Pleasant Company." Doll and paperback storybook - $82.00; outfit - $22.00. *Courtesy LeeAnn Geary.*

18" Molly McIntire from The American Girl Collection by the Pleasant Company. She is dressed in a separately purchased school outfit. Doll has vinyl head and limbs with cloth body, sleep eyes with lashes, and open/closed mouth with two teeth. Rooted hair is styled for braids or ponytails with back-stitched seam. She wears metal frame glasses with plastic lens. Doll is marked "© Pleasant Company" on back of neck. Doll and paperback book - $82.00; outfit - $20.00 *Courtesy LeeAnn Geary.*

12" Honey Tears was made by P.M. Sales (Paula Mae Dolls). She is made of vinyl with sleep eyes with lashes and rooted hair. Came on the market soon after Ideal introduced Tiny Tears, which turned out to be a very popular doll (1955–1962). All original. Mint condition - $35.00. *Courtesy Pat Graff.*

14" TRISHIE, one of the POSABLE PLAYMATES, made by Playmates in 1990. Has button eyes and rooted hair. She is very flexible. All original and in mint condition. $18.00. *Courtesy Pat Graff.*

16½" STEPHANIE made by Playwell in 1992. Made of vinyl with cloth body, sleep eyes with lashes, and rooted hair. Original and in mint condition. $25.00. *Courtesy Pat Graff.*

14" BARBRA STREISAND doll with excellent modeling and detail. She is made of vinyl with one-piece torso and legs. Neck and shoulders are jointed. Made in late 1960s by the Primrose Company, part of the Young & Fogg Co. of England. $100.00 up.

Raggedy Ann & Andy

The earliest Raggedy Ann & Andy dolls were made by cottage industry individuals hired by Johnny Gruelle and were very crude. These dolls have oil-painted features, brown yarn hair, tin or wooden eyes, a very thin nose, eyelashes painted well below the eyes, and no white outline around eyes. Some will have sewn "joints" at elbows and knees. Dolls will be marked "Patented Sept. 7, 1915."

In 1920 to 1934 the P.F. Volland Company made the Raggedy dolls. These dolls have features very much as the early dolls. The feet on these dolls seem to turn outward and some have rather large free standing thumbs, long thin noses and various mouth styles.

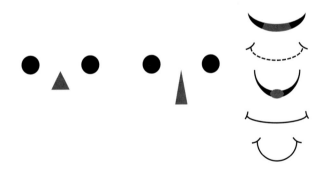

Mollye Doll Outfitters changed the entire concept of the dolls. They have a handwritten mark on the front torso, "Raggedy Ann and Andy Doll/Manufactured by Mollye Doll Outfitters." Mollye was the first to use solid red hearts printed on the chests. Another feature was black outlined noses for the dolls. (For more information, see under the Mollye section.)

Georgene Averill made Raggedy Ann & Andy from 1938 to the 1950s. They will have a label sewn to the seam of the doll and will have black outlined noses, but thousands were made without the outline.

Knickerbocker Toy Co. took over making the Raggedys from 1963 to 1982. They will have a tag sewn into a seam.

From 1981 to 1983, the Applause Toy Company made these dolls, and then Hasbro Company began their production in 1983. They are currently the manufacturer for the Raggedy dolls.

For additional Raggedy Ann & Andy information, see the following:

Modern Collector Dolls, Volume 7, page 222

Patricia Smith's Doll Values, Tenth Series, page 274

Patricia Smith's Doll Values, Eleventh Series, page 260

ANDREW TABBAT

237

On the left is a 15" RAGGEDY ANN made by Georgene Averill. The 18" doll on the right looks very commerical, but could have been home made. If it is a commerical doll, it most likely is an early Georgene Averill. 15" - $250.00 up. 18" - $100.00 up.

21" RAGGEDY ANN from 1953, maker unknown. Her eyes are faceted and not the usual smooth surface. She is holding 7" RAGGEDY ANN AND ANDY dolls made by Knickerbocker. 21" - $125.00 up; 7" - $65.00 each. *Courtesy Virginia Sofie.*

12" bean bag style RAGGEDY ANN AND ANDY made by Knickerbocker in the 1970s. Both are all original. Far left are copies made from felt, maker unknown. Each - $25.00. *Courtesy Gloria Woods.*

16" BEDTIME RAGGEDY ANN made in the 1980s by Knickerbocker. Made of cloth with painted features. Dress bib has red heart with "I Love You" printed on it. Dress tagged "Bedtime Raggedy Ann/Knickerbocker Toy Co. Inc." All original. $85.00 up.

20" FLOPPY FLO and JOLLY JOE made by My Toy Co. in the 1960s. Made of plush material. They are cute RAGGEDY ANN AND ANDY look-a-likes. Each - $25.00. *Courtesy Ellen Dodge.*

These seven 4½" RAGGEDY ANDY dolls came in basket. Each have glued-on clothes and a paper tag with a day of the week adhered to the clothes. They are poorly made and the maker is unknown. Made in 1972. Set - $30.00. *Courtesy Jo Keelen.*

7¾" JESUS is a full action figure with good modeling to face, beard, and hair. Has painted features and molded torso. Made by Rainfall and sold through religious goods stores. Original - $25.00.

Right: 12" GOLITH is a full action figure with excellent modeling to his mean face. He has a large nose, an open/closed mouth with two rows of painted teeth, a molded torso, and a molded-on crown. Clothes are removable. Left: 7¾" DAVID is also a full action figure with molded torso and sandals. Outfit comes with pouch and slingshot. Both are all original. GOLITH - $40.00. DAVID - $25.00.

⤳ Richwood ⤳

There is new information about Richwood Enterprises Company. Some of the dolls marked "Made in USA/14" were made for them, but they dressed and marketed them. These dolls were named Cindy Lou, and they were advertised as having "Round the Clock Fashions." She looks just like a Mary Hoyer doll.

For more information about this company and Sandra Sue dolls, see *Modern Collector Dolls, Volume 7,* page 225.

These four SANDRA SUE dolls are all original. She is shown with her walnut bed and wardrobe that was scaled to her size. SANDRA SUE had a vast wardrobe that could be purchased separately. Dolls - $100.00–165.00 each. Bed or wardrobe - $185.00 up. *Courtesy Marion Schmuhl.*

Sandra Sue with high heel feet dressed in outfit #F-70, "Sophisticated Evening." All original - $165.00. *Courtesy Maureen Fukushima.*

12" Peter Pan and Wendy made by Royal House of Dolls in 1989. Both are made of vinyl with rooted hair and sleep eyes with lashes. They are original and in mint condition. Each - $165.00. *Courtesy Pat Graff.*

14" Sweet Kimberly made exclusively for Hobby House Toys by Royal House of Dolls in 1989. She is a very pretty doll made of vinyl with sleep eyes and lashes. Limited to 250 pieces. $145.00. *Courtesy Pat Graff.*

12" JUNE was made by Royal House of Dolls in 1987. She has a wig and sleep eyes with lashes. $62.00 up. *Courtesy Pat Graff.*

12" CONSTANCE was made by Royal House of Dolls in 1986 and is part of the ROYAL COURT COLLECTION. She has sleep eyes with lashes. $62.00 up. *Courtesy Pat Graff.*

16" SUSIE was made by Royal House of Dolls in 1989. Made of all vinyl with rooted hair and sleep eyes with lashes. Original and in mint condition. $50.00. *Courtesy Pat Graff.*

21" SUZANNE was made by Royal House of Dolls in 1960. She has a ball-jointed waist and sleep eyes. This one is mint with box in unplayed condition. Tag says "costumed by Miss Rose of Royal." A red-haired version was made named POLLY. (It must be noted that parts and entire molds were sold to various companies, and this doll seems to have been passed on, with parts and pieces at several doll assembling companies.) $200.00 up. *Courtesy Pat Graff.*

This wonderfully mint and unplayed with doll was made by Royal in the 1950s. She is made of vinyl with rooted hair – not one strand out of place! She has medium high heels with original ballerina slippers. Original. In this con-dition - $225.00. Played with - $85.00 up. *Courtesy Diane Kornhauser.*

Early SASHA made by Trenton of England in 1969. Has very dark tan. Wrist tag says her name is SARA. $200.00 up. *Courtesy Linda Shelton.*

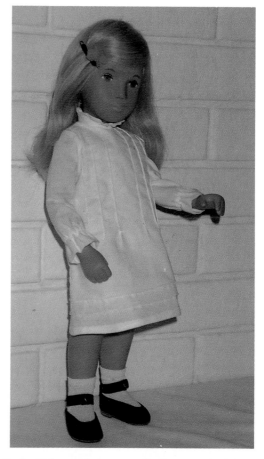

Limited edition 16" SASHA called PINTUCKS from 1982. All original. $285.00 up. *Courtesy Pat Graff.*

16" KILTIE is a limited edition SASHA from 1983. She has very pale blue painted eyes. All original and in mint condition. $300.00 up. *Courtesy Pat Graff.*

These thin 7½" dolls look exactly like 16" SASHA dolls. Box is only marked "Moni Dolls Poupes Puppen," and the dolls are unmarked. They were on the market for a few months around 1982. If found, they look cute with the real SASHA dolls holding them. Each - $20.00.

THE LOVABLES were made by Sayco in 1959 and consisted of 17½" mother, 9½" daughter, and 7½" baby. All are made of vinyl. Mother has sleep eyes, girl has inset eyes, and the baby has painted eyes. If marked, "Sayco" will be on head. That dark spot by girl's leg is the family dog, FIDO, made of all vinyl. Set - $95.00 up. *Courtesy Pat Graff.*

Left: 9½" O.J. SIMPSON dressed in original workout suit with his initials on front. Made by Shindana in 1976 at the height of his career. He also came in football outfit (see *Modern Collector Dolls, Volume 7*, page 233). $200.00 up. *Courtesy Phyllis Kates.*

Below: Accessory pack available in 1976 for the O.J. SIMPSON action figure. Raft, weights, track clothes, and jumping vaults. Not shown in right side of pack is the action figure dressed in football uniform. Pack alone - $30.00. With figure - $350.00.

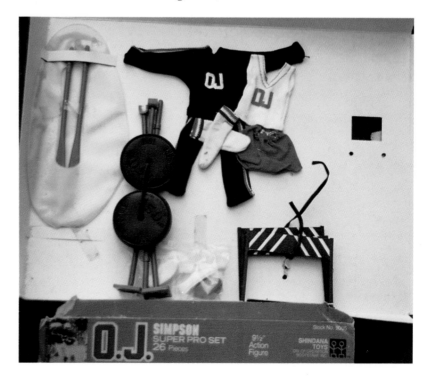

Rare 13" and 15" all celluloid dolls marked "SHIRLEY TEMPLE" on the neck. They do not have wigs, but do have a metal cap that is covered with lace. Each have an open/closed mouth, sleep eyes, and dimples. These two doll originally came from Holland and were once owned by Josie Vasquez and Angie Gonzales. 13" - $800.00; 15" - $900.00. *Courtesy Amanda Hash.*

18" all composition SHIRLEY TEMPLE dressed in Scotty dog dress. It's unusual because it came with a hat. Marked on head and body. $965.00. *Courtesy Jo Keelen.*

Both of these 27" SHIRLEY TEMPLE dolls have flirty eyes and are wearing original dresses. They are in near mint condition. Each - $1,400.00. *Courtesy Susan Girardot.*

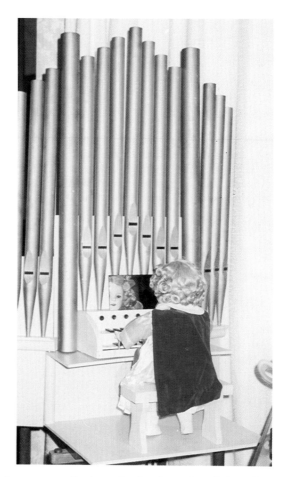

Mechanical 15" SHIRLEY TEMPLE plays the pipe organ. Rods are attached to the keyboard and into her composition hands. Motor-driven hands move across the keyboard. This item was made by Herbert O. Brown of Fairfield, Maine, in 1936, and was used in theater lobbies. $5,000.00 up. *Courtesy Martha Sweeney.*

All of these Shirley Temple accessory items are from the 1930s. Left to right: Ring from Brazil - $100.00 up. Celluloid pin - $165.00 up. Pink headband - $225.00 up. Hair holders/clasps - $185.00.
Courtesy Martha Sweeney.

12½", 6", and 14½" SHIRLEY TEMPLE chalk figurines from the 1930s. Larger ones were usually given away at carnivals. 12½" - $275.00, 6" - $185.00, 14½" - $300.00. *Courtesy Martha Sweeney.*

Box with six Shirley Temple mugs from the 1930s. One was given away with Bisquick purchase. This is how the mugs were shipped to the grocery stores. Set - $425.00. *Courtesy Pat Sparks.*

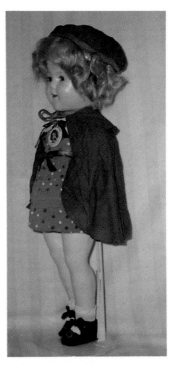

6½ x7¼" plaster plaque with Shirley Temple's name on bottom edge. Top edge is marked "Aug. Mack Bedford Ind. 1937." $165.00 up. *Courtesy Martha Sweeney.*

Navy rubber lined rain cape and beret made for SHIRLEY TEMPLE in 1936. Designed and made for Ideal Doll Company by Mollye Goldman. 20" - $1,100.00. *Courtesy Martha Sweeney.*

SHIRLEY TEMPLE cloth rain cape, hat, and umbrella in a delightful print. Cape is tagged. In mint condition, from 1930s. $200.00. *Courtesy Jo Keelen.*

Shirley Temple "Cinderella" dresses for girls from 1930s. Each - $85.00 up. *Courtesy Pat Sparks and Lea Nell Hayes.*

More Shirley Temple "Cinderella" dresses from the 1930s. Each - $85.00 up. *Courtesy Pat Sparks and Lea Nell Hayes.*

Right: Cinderella frock with Shirley Temple tag, size 8. $85.00 up.

Courtesy Pat Sparks and Lea Nell Hayes.

16" SWEET LOVE made by Straco in 1990. Made of vinyl with cloth body, sleep eyes, and rooted hair. All original. $18.00. *Courtesy Pat Graff.*

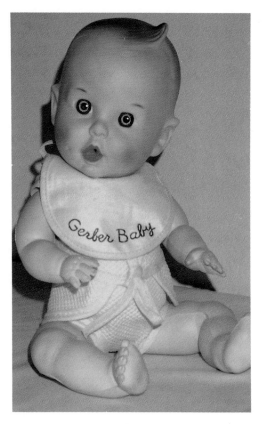
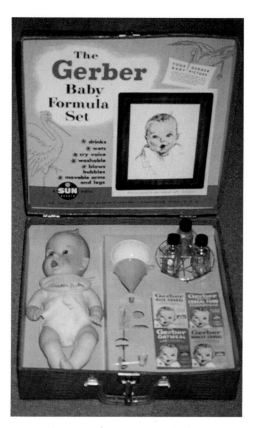

12" GERBER BABY with case from 1954. Has vinyl head with all rubber body. Wearing original clothes. Marked "Gerber Baby/Gerber Products Co." on head and "Mfg. by/The Sun Rubber Co./Barberton, O USA/Pat. 2118682/Pat. 2160739" on back. Doll and case are in mint condition. Doll only, mint condition - $95.00. Mint in case - $200.00. *Courtesy Jo Keelen.*

16" TERRI LEE and 10" TINY TERRI LEE have the same style dresses but the imprinted materials are different. Yet, both materials have monkeys imprinted on them. TERRI LEE has an unusual eye color that can not be seen in this photograph. It has been reported that one artist at the TERRI LEE manufacturing plant painted eyes a light pastel color instead of dark brown. TINY TERRI LEE has sleep eyes. 16" - $450.00. 10" - $200.00. *Courtesy Cyndie Matus.*

16" TERRI LEE and 10" TINY TERRI LEE are dressed in matching dresses, and what a cute pair they are! TERRI LEE is a talker with Swiss fiber hair and was distributed by Mar-Fan, Inc. TERRI LEE talkers did come with these vinyl slip-on shoes with no socks. TINY TERRI LEE still has her factory-issued daisy that is tied to her wrist. 16", mint condition - $575.00. 10" - $225.00. *Courtesy Susan Girardot.*

16" TERRI LEE wearing all original #540A pique suit. Has original wrist tag and daisy tied to wrist. She also has her original box. In this condition - $475.00. *Courtesy June Schultz.*

16" TERRI LEE dressed in original Irish costume, except for replaced hat. $400.00. *Coutesy June Schultz.*

16" TERRI LEE in a cute skater's costume. In near mint condition. $450.00. *Courtesy Kris Lundquist.*

10" TINY TERRI and JERRI LEE are dressed in all original nurse and sailor outfits. JERRI LEE has unusal platinum caracul wig. TERRI LEE has a saran wig. Nurse - $265.00. Sailor - $325.00. *Courtesy Cyndie Matus.*

⮞ Thin Plastic Dolls ⮜

"Thin plastic" is the only description that can be used for this style doll. Occasionally, they are mistaken for celluloid dolls because of their see-through thinness and extremely light weight. It's a shame that they are considered poor quality dolls, because many of them have more "personality" than some of the good quality dolls. Yet when you get several of the thin plastic dolls together and compare, they do not look so bad. They may never achieve a high value, but they "hold their own" for uniqueness.

Most thin plastic dolls were made in Hong Kong with a small number being made in Japan. If marked, a registration number can be found followed by "Made in Hong Kong" and the symbol of "M" over "PF" in a circle. This maker is Mag-Jongg (Pau-Fong).

Many of these dolls have excellent design and modeling, but often times the seam lines have not been cleaned off. Also, the dolls have glued-on or stapled-on clothes. Some will have painted eyes, but most have inset glassene eyes.

These attractive thin plastic dolls are 20", 19", and 17" tall. They have great hair styling, and all have been re-dressed. Two have adult figures, and the center doll has high heel feet. 17" - $30.00. 19" - $35.00. 20" - $40.00. *Courtesy Randy Numley.*

Left: 14" nurse with non-removable clothes, inset eyes and medium heeled feet. Right: 14½" doll made of more conventional vinyl. Has tightly rooted hair and high heel feet. 14" - $25.00. 14½" - $32.00. *Courtesy Randy Numley.*

This 13½" young lady is rather buxom looking! She has inset glassene eyes and high heel feet. Re-dressed nicely. $30.00. *Courtesy Randy Numley.*

4" and 5½" thin plastic dolls with adult figures. Both have hair molded very much alike. Both have bra tops, but torso and leg construction is different. Taller doll has sleep eyes; smaller one, painted eyes. 4" - $3.00. 5½" - $6.00. *Courtesy Randy Numley.*

Left: 11½" LILLI-type made of thin plastic. The pony-tail rotates, and eye makeup is very heavy. She has high heels. $45.00. *Courtesy Randy Numley.*

Right: 12" thin plastic doctor with inset glassene eyes and non-removable clothes. Has excellent quality modeling. $20.00. *Courtesy Randy Numley.*

8" thin plastic boy with large glassene inset eyes. Note the seam lines have not been cleaned off. $12.00. *Courtesy Randy Numley.*

5" little boy with molded-on clothes and eyes painted to the side. He is jointed at shoulders only. $6.00. *Courtesy Randy Numley.*

Left: 19" all original nurse and baby made of thin plastic. Has non-removable clothes, excellent hairdo, and glassene eyes. $30.00. *Courtesy Randy Numley.*

Right: 19" doctor with non-removable clothes, side part molded hairdo, painted eyes, and molded-on shoes. It's amazing how tight this company glued the shirt on. $35.00. *Courtesy Randy Numley.*

17" adult lady with high heeled feet, detailed hands, and large glassene eyes. $28.00. *Courtesy Randy Numley.*

7" child nurse with glued-on clothes, molded hair, and glassene eyes. Shoes and socks are molded-on. $18.00. *Courtesy Randy Numley.*

11½" nurse and doctor with molded-on underwear, non-removable clothes, and glassene eyes. They are jointed at neck and shoulders only. **Each - $18.00.** *Courtesy Randy Numley.*

17" nurse with glued-on clothes, medium heeled feet, and glassene inset eyes. **$20.00.** *Courtesy Randy Numley.*

16" girl with glassene inset eyes. Note unusual hairdo. She has been re-dressed. **$18.00.** *Courtesy Randy Numley.*

11½" little girl with glassene eyes and molded-on shoes and socks. She has been re-dressed. $22.00. *Courtesy Randy Numley.*

This shows a 19" thin plastic doll with a cryer box inserted in its back. A large number of adult, toddler, and baby dolls came with these noise boxes. (Italian dollmakers made similar dolls.) This doll has a great hairdo. $30.00. *Courtesy Randy Numley.*

MARY JANE has a vinyl head, sleep eyes, painted hard plastic body, and original tagged panties. She was made by Togs & Toys. MARY JANE's wrist tag advertises her Celenese acetate plastic construction and her 36 available outfits. In this condition - $350.00. *Courtesy Susan Girardot.*

17" KIMBERLY made by Tomy in 1984. Dressed in separate boxed soccer outfit. $65.00. *Courtesy Pat Graff.*

19" MOTHER has cloth body with vinyl ¾ arms and legs. Vinyl head has painted features and rooted nylon hair. She has molded-on wedding ring, high heels, and excellent quality removable clothes. Body is tagged "Mommy Doll/Tootsietoy. C.J. Design 1990." Head marked "1990 C.J. Design, Inc./Tootsietoy." Her 6" BABY is made of full-jointed vinyl with painted features, dimples, and widespread fingers. Head marked "D/C Designs, Inc./1987." Set - $40.00.

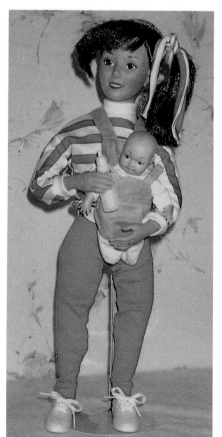

19" MOMMY DOLL - ON THE GO was a later issue made by Tootsietoy in 1992. Both dolls are made of vinyl with cloth bodies and have painted features. Mommy has rooted hair. All original. $40.00. *Courtesy Pat Graff.*

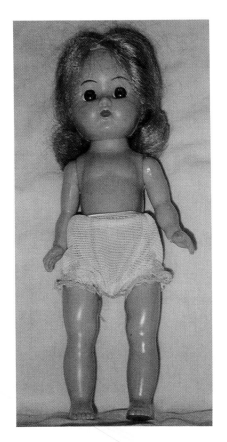

This 7½" GINGER made by Cosmopolition was sold as a blank doll to Totsy Mfg. Co. who dressed and marketed the doll as LITTLE MISS TOTSY. When sold in this box, the doll came dressed in panties, shoes, and socks (missing). It has not been verified if the doll was ever sold dressed or if the clothes were available separately. Original price tag is 88¢. $135.00. *Courtesy Carl Jankech.*

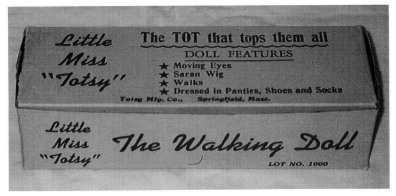

This inexpensively made, all composition doll was made in 1932 by the Toy Products Mfg. Co. for Hoster Marketing of Newark, N.J. Doll has been re-dressed. Original clothes were often stapled on. She is a PATSY-type doll but lacks the bent right arm at elbow. She can also be identified by her downcast eyebrows. Hoster actually marketed the dolls/ statues through carnival supply houses. Dolls were sold at boardwalk stands in Atlantic City and on Coney Island. $45.00. *Courtesy David Spurgeon.*

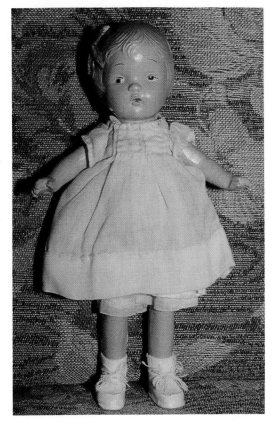

ᵒᵉ Uneeda ᵉᵒ

Uneeda has been at the lower end of the doll market for generations (since before the 1920s). This firm has never been a leader in the doll industry but has sustained by putting out more reasonably priced dolls than their big-time competitors – the majority of which have gone out of business. Many of Uneeda's dolls are look-alikes of other manufacturer's dolls. They also made a number of dolls that are considered highly collectible now. When found in mint condition, these dolls can command high prices for non-babies.

10¼" SUZETTE is made of all vinyl with high-heeled feet and swivel waist. Has three painted lashes at sides of eyes. Dressed in original bride outfit. Marked "Uneeda" on head. $65.00 up. *Courtesy Marie Ernst.*

16" COQUETTE BRIDE was made by Uneeda from 1961 through 1967. Made of plastic and vinyl with sleep eyes and rooted hair. Marked either "1961" or "1963" (slight mold changes made in 1963.) $32.00. *Courtesy Kathy Trvdik.*

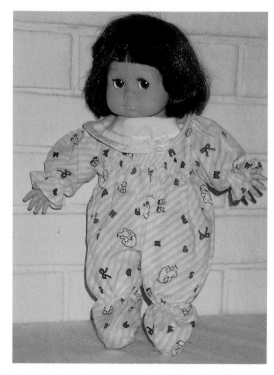

14" I LOVE YOU DOLLY was made by Uneeda in 1989. Made of vinyl with cloth body, inset eyes with lashes. Eyes "follow" you as *you* move from side to side. $15.00. *Courtesy Pat Graff.*

10" POLLYANNA (left) is the same doll as SUZETTE (right) except she does not have a swivel waist. Both have high-heeled feet and three lashes painted to side of their eyes. They are shown with extra outfits. They are marked "Uneeda" on their backs. SUZETTE was also marketed as TINYTEEN and the BLUE FAIRY from Disney's *Pinocchio.* $65.00 up. *Courtesy Marie Ernst.*

19" LUCETA made by Vicma in 1988. She is made of vinyl with cloth body, inset eyes, heavy lashes, and applied boots with small heels. All original. $40.00.

Courtesy Pat Graff.

Vogue

Below is a brief outline of dolls marketed by Vogue and their estimated value.

Toodles: (1948–1949) All composition. $400.00.
Ginny: (1950–1953) Hard plastic, strung, painted eyes. $350.00.
Ginny: (1950–1953) Hard plastic, strung, sleep eyes, painted lashes. $350.00.
Ginny: (1950–1953) Child (not baby), caracul (lamb's wool) wig. $375.00.
Ginny: (1954) Hard plastic walker, sleep eyes, painted lashes. $275.00.
Ginny: (1955–1957) Hard plastic walker, molded lashes. $185.00.
Ginny: (1957–1962) Hard plastic walker, jointed knees, molded lashes. $150.00.
Ginny Crib Crowd: Bent limb baby body, caracul (lamb's wool) wig. $600.00 up.
Ginny: (1977) All vinyl with round face. $50.00 up.
Internationals: $45.00 up.
Sasson Ginny: (1978–1979) Thin-bodied doll with thin limbs, sleep eyes. $28.00. With painted eyes: $32.00.

8" TODDLES **is made of all composition and is all original. From 1948–1949. $375.00 up.** *Courtesy Ellen Dodge.*

Expectionally pretty 8" GINNY **from the 1952 series. All original. $325.00 up.** *Courtesy Susan Girardot.*

8" FAIRY GODMOTHER **from 1950 to 1953. Made of all hard plastic with painted eyes. All original in original box. $325.00 up.** *Courtesy Kris Lundquist.*

DEBUTANTE SERIES GINNY dolls from 1950s. Both are all original and in mint condition. $325.00 up. *Courtesy Margaret Mandel.*

This doll is from TINY MISS GINNY series of 1952. She has a caracul wig. This is the same doll as the CRIB CROWD babies. All original and in mint condition. $325.00 up.
Courtesy Margaret Mandel.

Beautiful RODEO GIRL GINNY from 1952. Outfit is not faded but has very vivid colors. All original. $325.00 up. *Courtesy Margaret Mandel.*

FUNTIME GINNY from 1954. She is all original and in mint condition. $325.00 up. *Courtesy Margaret Mandel.*

Really cute all hard plastic COWGIRL GINNY from 1957. All original and in mint condition. $300.00 up.

Courtesy Kris Lundquist.

GINNY SPORTS SERIES from 1958. All original and in very mint condition. $300.00 up. *Courtesy Margaret Mandel.*

8" all vinyl GINNY dolls in international costumes. They date from 1965 and are shown in original boxes. $45.00 up. *Courtesy Kris Lundquist.*

This all vinyl GINNY was made in 1984 while molds and rights still belonged to Meritus. Early 1980s vinyl may turn "sweaty" if kept in the box. All original - $25.00 up.

All vinyl SASSON GINNY from 1978. All original. Marked "4/Ginny/Vogue Dolls/1977" on head and "1978 Vogue Dolls, Inc./Made in Hong Kong" on body. $35.00 up.

JILL wearing original "after 5" dress. Ribbon has been added to hair. From 1960. $175.00 up. *Courtesy Maureen Fukushima.*

JILL is wearing a very nice coat and matching hat with "fur" trim. From 1960. $175.00 up. *Courtesy Maureen Fukushima.*

All hard plastic JILL dressed in very attractive #7514 outfit. All original, from 1959. $175.00 up.

Courtesy Maureen Fukushima.

This 1959 JILL makes a very pretty bride. She is all original. $175.00 up. *Courtesy Maureen Fukushima.*

This 1959 JILL, wearing pretty #7501 dress, has a problem with her hose! $175.00 up. *Courtesy Maureen Fukushima.*

1959 JILL in all original playsuit, #3417. $175.00 up.

Courtesy Maureen Fukushima.

This is a 1958 JILL dressed in coat and hat outfit, #3395. $175.00 up. *Courtesy Maureen Fukushima.*

10" JILL in a beautiful outfit #3199 from 1958. $175.00 up. *Courtesy Maureen Fukushima.*

Basic JILL in outfit #3300-7561. She is made of all hard plastic with jointed knees, sleep eyes, molded eyelashes, painted fingernails, and high heel feet. Marked "Vogue" on head and "Jill/Vogue/Made in USA 1957" on body. $200.00 up. *Courtesy Maureen Fukushima.*

10" all vinyl JAN with vinyl head with almost a smile mouth. Dressed in original 1958 coat and glasses. $185.00 up. *Courtesy Maureen Fukushima.*

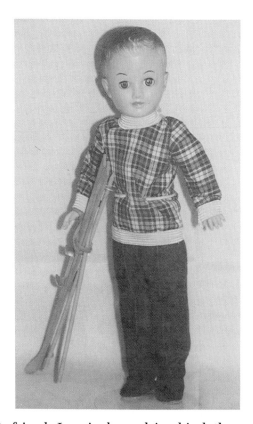

10" all vinyl JAN has straight legs, swivel waist, high heel feet, rooted saran hair, almost a smile mouth, sleep eyes with three painted lashes to sides, and molded lashes. Marked "Vogue." Made from 1958 to 1962. $185.00. *Courtesy Maureen Fukushima.*

JILL's friend, JEFF, is dressed in ski clothes minus the jacket. He is made of plastic and vinyl with sleep eyes and molded hair. From 1957. $95.00. *Courtesy Maureen Fukushima.*

Left: Unknown young adult marked "Vogue" on back of head. She has vinyl head with rooted hair, vinyl arms, and plastic body and legs. Her sleep eyes have molded lashes with three painted lashes to side of eyes. She is a very pretty young lady that dates from approximately 1963–1965. Not dressed in original clothes. $85.00 up.

Right: 14" plastic and vinyl BRIDE uses the MISS GINNY doll. She has rooted hair and sleep eyes. Original. $45.00. *Courtesy Kathy Tvrdik.*

16" all vinyl GINNY BABY wearing original dress. She has sleep eyes and open mouth/nurser. Dates from 1969. $30.00. *Courtesy Pat Graff.*

15" LITTLEST ANGEL made of plastic and vinyl. Dress is tagged "Vogue Dolls, Inc./Made in U.S.A." and head marked "1965." Box marked "Vogue Dolls/Subsidiary of Tonka Corp." $35.00. *Courtesy Marie Ernst.*

BOBBI-MAE, THE SWING & SWAY DOLL was made by Wondercraft in 1940 and was inspired by Sammy Kaye and his Swing and Sway Orchestra. She is constructed of composition, and when swaying, the head goes in the opposite direction to the body. In mint condition - $165.00 up. *Courtesy Kay Bransky.*

8" CARA - LINES AND SQUARE is made of vinyl with painted eyes. All original from 1990. $70.00. *Courtesy Pat Graff.*

8" CHRISTOPHER ROBIN - VESPERS is made of vinyl with painted eyes. All original from 1990. $100.00. *Courtesy Pat Graff.*

8" EMMALINE - BEFORE TEA is made of vinyl with painted features. All original from 1990. $75.00. *Courtesy Pat Graff.*

8" JANE - THE GOOD LITTLE GIRL is made of vinyl with painted features. All original from 1990. $70.00. *Courtesy Pat Graff.*

8" FRANCIE - DOWN BY THE POND has painted features. All original from 1990. $80.00. *Courtesy Pat Graff.*

14" CHELSEA GOES TO THE FAIR has green painted eyes and carries a quilt. From 1991. $145.00 *Courtesy Pat Graff.*

21" RACHAEL - SUMMER WEDDING was sculpted by Abigail Brahms and limited to 250. She has painted features. All original. $450.00. *Courtesy Pat Graff.*

18" porcelain ELVIS made by World Dolls in the 1980s. It has been reported that only 300 of these very special dolls were made. What makes this doll special are the Elvis Presley "tour belt" replica and the "TCB" (Taking Care of Business) initaled ring. (The phrase was a favorite of Elvis, and the initials can be found on many of his personal items.) The neckpiece is also a copy of one owned by Elvis. $775.00 up.

Courtesy Claudia Meeker.

⁓ Bibliography ⁓
Selected References

CATALOGS, NEWSPAPERS, MAGAZINES

Alexander, Madame, 1934–1941 (newspaper/magazines) 1942–1943, 1950–1995

Alexander, Madame Doll Club Review Magazine

Altman's Catalogs, 1958, 1960–1965

Annalee Society: Newsletter from Annalee Society

Bennett Bros. Wholesale Catalogs, 1953–1969

Butler Bros. Catalogs, 1933–1938

Coast to Coast: Catalogs and flyers, 1949–1957, 1959–1963

Walt Disney, Archives, Reports, 1938–1940. Catalogs, 1987–1994

Doll Castle News, July, August 1968.

Effanbee Doll Co. Catalogs, 1949–1959, 1966–1971, 1974–1983, 1994

FAO Schwarz Catalogs, 1942–1954,1976, 1978–1994

Fortune Magazine, Dec. 1936, Oct. 1940

Hagns Catalog, 1941–1949

Himstedt Times Newsletter, Vols, 4–11

Holiday Gift Catalog, 1942–1945

Naber Kids Newsletter, 1994–1995

National Bella Hess Catalogs, 1948–1970

Macy Catalog, 1960

Miller Barbie Collector Magazine, 1995

Montgomery Wards, 1918–1994

McCall Needlework Magazine, Fall/Winter 1952–1953

Nirisk Catalogs, 1952–1959

Philadelphia Inquirer Newspaper, Dec. 1967, Aug., Oct., Nov., 1969.

Playthings Magazines, Feb 1932–1940, 1943–1995

Plain, John, Wholesale Catalogs, 1940s to 1954

Remco Co. Catalogs, 1963–1967

Rhode-Spencer Catalogs, 1934–1946

Sears Roebuck Catalogs, 1932–1994

Slack Mfg. Co., 1940–1943

Time & Toys Catalog, 1958–1960

Toyland Catalog, 1957, 1960

Toy and Novelties Magazine, May 1946–Jan. 1976

Toy Yearbook, 1949–1957

Topper Toy Co. Catalogs, 1961–1965

Uneeda Co. Catalogs, 1964–1970

John Wanamaker Catalogs, 1950–1953

Western Auto Supply Catalogs, 1946–1954, 1957–196?

Woolworth Flyers/Catalogs, 1950–1957

Women's Home Companion Magazine, Dec. 1946–Dec. 1957

BOOKS

Anderton, Johana. *Twentieth Century Dolls, Vol. 1 & 2*

Axe, John. *Effanbee: A Collector's Encyclopedia*

Axe, John. *Encyclopedia of Celebrity Dolls*

Brooks, Tim & Marsh, Earle. *The Complete Directory To Prime Time Network TV Shows, 1948 to present*

Bourgeois, Joe. *Dolls in Uniform*

Burdick, Lorraine. *Celebrity Doll Journal, Child Dolls & Toys*

Colemans, Dorothy, Elizabeth, Evelyn. *The Collector's Encyclopedia of Dolls, Vol. 2.*

Directory of United States Trademarks

Eames, Sarah Sink. *Barbie Fashions*

Gibbs, Patikii. *Horsman Dolls 1950-1970.*

Hoyer, Mary. *Mary Hoyer Dolls*

Izen, Judith. *Collector's Guide to Ideal Dolls*

Judd, Polly & Pam. *Hard Plastic Dolls, Vol. 1 & 2; Glamour Dolls 1950s-1960s, Composition Dolls, Vol. 1 & 2, Cloth Dolls*

Nieswonger, Jennie. *That Doll Ginny*

Perkins, Myla. *Black Dolls, Vol. 1 & 2*

Robison, Joleen & Sellers, Kay. *Advertising Dolls*

Index